contents

cover design by Jonathan Green-Armytage. Printed and bound by Civic Press Limited (TU), Civic Street, Glasgow, C.4. SBN 7163 4010 0 (cloth), 7163 4011 9 (paper).

the fifth social service:
a critical analysis
of the Seebohm proposals

this book, like all publications of the Fabian Society, repre-
sents not the collective view of the Society but only the
view of the individuals who prepared it. The responsibility of
the Society is limited to approving the publications which it
issues as worthy of consideration within the Labour movement. Fabian Society, 11 Dartmouth Street, London SW1.
May 1970

1. the objectives of the new local social service

Peter Townsend

This book expresses the need for a new theory of community development and for a new departure in social policy. It had its origins in a conference called by the Fabian Society on 1 February 1969 to discuss the Seebohm Report (*Report of the Committee on Local Authority and Allied Personal Social Services*), which had been published in July 1968. A number of the chapters in this book were presented at this conference, but some have been extensively revised and other chapters have been written subsequently. The final preparation of the manuscript for the press was deliberately held up until the Government announced its reaction to the Seebohm Report. On 12 February 1970 the Local Authority Services Bill was published and on 26 February the bill was given a second reading in Parliament. In the same month the Government announced its reactions to the Redcliffe-Maud Commission on Local Government (*Reform of Local Government in England*, Cmnd 4276, London, HMSO) and published a green paper on the health service (DHSS, *National Health Service: The future structure of the* NHS, London, HMSO). This book therefore examines and discusses the development of local social services within the new administrative framework that is envisaged.

The broad conclusion illustrated in different ways by several authors in this book can be put briefly. The Seebohm Report is constructive and its chief recommendation to merge the local services in one department is justified. But as an example of planning the report is lacking in analysis, drive and vision and it gives an insufficient picture of the objectives that should be pursued. Partly as a consequence the Government's proposed legislation and its policy statements also lack these qualities. The last two sentences of the Government's explanatory and financial memorandum to the Local Authority Social Services Bill state " The Bill is therefore not expected to result in any significant increase in expenditure out of public funds. The Bill is not expected to have any appreciable overall effects on public service manpower requirements." If the Government had intended to deepen the misgivings of its critics it could not have found two better chosen sentences.

I shall attempt in this introduction to discuss the general issues raised by the Seebohm reform—whether the extent and kind of need has been ascertained; the objectives of the new department clearly formulated; its future structure and functions defined; and finally, a programme of priorities laid out to show how the objectives might be realistically fulfilled. Subsequent chapters will discuss the particular problems of housing and of services for children, the mentally handicapped and the aged. Two concluding chapters will be concerned with the political, professional and administrative changes required to protect welfare rights.

All planning must involve the formulation of objectives. The Seebohm committee was appointed on 20 December 1965 to " review the organisation and responsibilities of the local authority personal social services in England and Wales, and to consider what changes are desirable to secure an effective family service." The committee decided that these terms of reference allowed them to consider the needs of individuals and married couples as well as families and to inquire into the whole of the work of children's and welfare departments and those elements of the work of health, education and housing departments which were concerned with social work. The scope of the inquiry could therefore be widely drawn. Events in Scotland had moved more swiftly. The Kilbrandon Report in 1964 (Scottish Home and Health Department, *Children and Young Persons* (Scotland), Cmnd 2306, London, HMSO, 1964) led to a working group being set up which reported on reorganisation of services in 1966 (*Social Work and the Community: Proposals for Reorganising Local Authority Services in Scotland*, Cmnd 3605, London, HMSO, 1966). This resulted quickly in legislation.

How should the Seebohm committee have set about the job of defining policy objectives? There are a number of awkward alternatives. First, subjective opinions can be collected from both consumers and suppliers of services about the quality of existing services, how they might be improved in the future and what new services might be added. The comments of those with direct current experience of particular services can be illuminating but the comments of others may be largely meaningless. The opinions of individuals offer little guidance to the policy-maker unless they are founded on information and experience. Even then it is difficult to evaluate them without a knowledge of the social circumstances and situation of those expressing them. The same is true of subjective expressions of need. The individual may feel deprived even if others consider he has no cause to feel like this and even if there appear to be no objective criteria to justify his feeling. Equally, he may deny any need whatsoever and yet be destitute, ill or live in squalor. Subjective deprivation is subtle and hard to ascertain, because there are social rules and situations which govern whether or not and when it will be expressed, and yet this information is not superfluous. It is one bit of vital information in planning.

Second, there are conventional or social "views" or definitions of needs and standards of service. These too can be identified and collected. There are social norms about the upbringing of children, the care of the ill and the handicapped and the help that should be given to families who are poor. These are often implicit in behaviour, organisation and opinion rather than consciously formulated, and have to be analysed out. Sometimes they form the basis of law and regulation. For example, Government and local authority regulations embody social views about decent standards of housing and the point at which houses or flats are treated as overcrowded. Different societies (and indeed different sections of any single society) may define these standards differently but in principle the social scientist can measure the extent to which they are or are not met. He can help a society to understand how practice may differ from precept. How many in the population fall below the poverty line as defined socially by public assistance scales? How many are living in conditions treated by society as unsanitary or overcrowded? How many are in need of hospital care, residential care, sheltered housing, rehabilitation, special schooling, domiciliary service and so on, according to criteria implicit or explicit in laws and regulations and government policy statements? In examining social or normative definitions of need the social scientist can help to bring them into the open, reveal contradicitons and loose ends and show the different functions played by law, regulation, policy and custom. He can even show the degrees of efficiency with which different standards are being met and therefore suggest what might be gained with alternative emphases in policy.

This gives a rough outline of a two-stage procedure or model that might be followed in planning. Certainly we would have a basis for comparing subjective with collectively acknowledged need, and policy aims with policy achievements. He could pursue the connections between the rise of subjective deprivation in particular groups and professions, change in society's definition of need and change in society's services and practices.

But this would be insufficient as a basis for planning. Social policy would be viewed too much from within, psychologically and institutionally. Services would be judged too much in terms of objectives already defined than of those which have yet to be defined, too much in terms of needs already recognised, subjectively and socially, than of those which have still to be recognised. Standards and needs have to be judged also from some external standpoint. While ultimately it may be difficult to substantiate a true objectivity, nonetheless this goal is worth striving for. Needs can be shown to exist, independent of the feelings engendered within a particular society and independent of those which are recognised by society's institutions. Just as there is subjective deprivation and socially acknowledged deprivation, so there is objective deprivation. A man may not feel deprived and he may not even meet society's rules defining someone who is deprived and yet he may be shown to be deprived. He lacks what his fellows can be demonstrated to have and suffers in some tangible and measurable way as a consequence.

This would complete a three part model for the analysis of social policy and the production of policy objectives. But how could need be defined objectively? How could standards be evolved, independent of those that have been developed historically and which society recognises? The interconnections between the concepts of inequality and deprivation provide the best answer. Inequality has two aspects. There is inequality of resources: individuals and families fall into horizontal strata, according to their incomes, assets, fringe benefits received from employers, and benefits in kind received from the public social services. Through rigorous comparison between regions and communities as well as individuals and families the inequalities in the distribution of resources can be revealed in elaborate detail, including, for example, inequalities of space at home, working conditions and school facilities. There is also inequality of social integration: individuals, families and ethnic communities fall into vertical categories according to the degree of isolation or segregation from society. People vary in the density and range of their household, family, community and social networks; and some populations of hospitals and other institutions are extraordinarily isolated. There are inequalities of social support in illness, infirmity, disability and bereavement. While planning cannot make good private loss it can provide substitute and compensating services. Visiting services can be developed for the isolated elderly and home help services for the infirm and disabled. Services like teaching in English and information and legal aid services can also be developed as integrating mechanisms and protection against exploitation for immigrant communities.

Complementing these two measures of inequality would be measures of deprivation. In descending the scale of income or of other resources, such as assets, there is a point at which the individual's or the family's participation in the ordinary activities, customs and pleasures of the community is likely to fall off more sharply than the reduction of income. His opportunities to share in the pursuits and meet the needs enjoined by the culture become grossly restricted. As a consequence he may be malnourished, inadequately housed, disadvantaged in schooling, unable to use public services like buses and trains, and restricted to impoverished sectors of the social services. If he belongs to an ethnic group which feels itself to be cold-shouldered by external society and which responds by turning in upon its own improvised resources he runs the risk of being by-passed by new scientific and cultural developments, excluded from the ordinary range of information and com-munication media, ignorant of legal and welfare rights and left with the housing, the land and the commodities least desired by outsiders. If he is someone isolated from the community because he has not married, has been bereaved, has lost con-temporaries during the ageing process, has become separated from family and friends because of work or migration, is disabled or lives in a sparsely populated area, or is affected by a number of these factors, he may not be put in touch with health and welfare services at necessary times, may remain unaware of social developments (for example, rent rebate schemes, decimal coinage, new advances in reading and hearing aids) and *become* deprived and perhaps liable to exploitation even if not deprived beforehand. The interaction of the two kinds of inequality—poverty of resources and isolation—can have devastating consequences for some sections of the population during periods of rapid technological and institutional change.

Such is a possible framework of thought and analysis. How did the Seebohm Com-mittee proceed? First, subjective opinion. Through memoranda presented as evidence and through various consultations the committee learned the views of suppliers of services. The opinions of " all those concerned with the services " were felt to be important but the opinions of those utilising the services were not collected. " We were, regrettably, unable to sound consumer reaction to the services in any systematic fashion " (p 21). This decision was taken, the committee say, because a research programme would have delayed publication by a year or two. But the committee took $2\frac{1}{2}$ years to report, and the Government took a further 20 months to react to the report. Much research of value could have been launched, even if some of it could not have reached fruition until the months following the publication of the report. The gross lack of information about the nature and functions of the services covered by the committee and about consumer opinion, could hardly have gone unnoticed. The Younghusband Committee on local authority social workers had toiled for $3\frac{1}{2}$ years in the late 1950s and had dared to conclude " We should like to have undertaken a complementary inquiry into the reactions of those using the services. An investigation of this nature would, however, have prolonged our own inquiries unduly." And they went on, " We were struck . . . by the lack of any systematic study of the part played by social workers in meeting needs within the framework of the social services. Such information could have had an important bearing on our own inquiry. We should like to draw attention to the desirability of such study. We think much of the confusion in regard to the functions of social workers in the health and welfare services, as elsewhere, is due to lack of analyses of this kind." (*Report of the Working Party on Social Workers in the Local Authority Health and Welfare Services*, pp 2-3, London, HMSO, 1959).

But the Seebohm Committee appear to have ignored this recommendation and failed to clear up the confusion. Other committees have instigated and brought to a successful culmination very large research inquiries within a similar time span. The Robbins Committee on Higher Education, for example, had launched a very ambitious research programme and yet had reported within two and a half years.

The implications of failing to find out consumer opinion run deep. Some far-reaching criticisms of professional activity may be either undetected or under-estimated. Some needs which are felt by individuals or groups may be ignored. Most important, some of the rights of the consumer to a voice in planning and administration may be unrecognised.

social standards

The Seebohm Committee did in fact go some way towards fulfilling the second and third parts of our planning model. They attempted to present conventional views on needs and standards of service. They also attempted to collate statistics giving objective measures of need. However, such secondary analysis as was carried out was neither complete nor consistent.

For example, insufficient effort was made to define the criteria by which people are helped by the existing services and to subject these to searching examination. A rather haphazard collection of over a hundred pages of appendices attached to the Committee's report contain chiefly an account of administrative structure and statistics, and the data are not digested and integrated with the argument in the body of the text. What are existing standards of service? Which children are taken into care and why? How are homeless families defined in practice, and is it logical to exclude single persons and married couples from services? Which disabled persons are placed on registers and how does this vary among the different areas of the country? These are the kinds of question which have to be answered in detail if the standards of service which prevail at present are to be delineated.

Again, the attempts to measure objectively the extent of unmet need were very clumsy. Such attempts can determine the conclusions which may be reached not only about the *structure* but also the *scale* and *scope* of a future service. Thus it is vital to ask whether there are any important needs which are totally unmet at present and for which new social services might be developed. In terms of possible contribution to social integration there might be a public radio-telephone service and a transport service for certain disabled or elderly persons and their relatives and friends; an architect and design service for do-it-yourself enthusiasts; a mobile national housing repairs and improvement squad; neighbourhood and home tuition in speaking and writing English for immigrant families and handicapped pupils; and a shopping and sightseeing touring service for the hospitalised and infirm. Only by systematic study of social inequalities, comparing the circumstances of different families and individuals and comparing the real functions of the social services with implicit as well as explicit social objectives can these lacunae be revealed. The Seebohm Committee did not produce guidelines for fresh developments in social policy as a result of analysing social conditions and policies.

However, it did not measure possible developments in existing services either. Chapters on services for children, old people, the physically handicapped, the mentally ill and subnormal, other local health services and housing seem to have been allocated to different authors. This must partly explain their uneven quality. Some of these neglect valuable sources of information. For example, there is no analysis of trends in the development of services in relation to previous and prospective changes in population structure (as in D. Paige and K. Jones, *Health and Welfare Services in Britain in 1975*, Cambridge University Press, 1966). Some chapters, like that on old people, mix the trivial with the crucial as if they were of equal importance. Present shortcomings are, however, emphasised. But they are

reason
why
development slow
Recommendation

emphasised without corresponding documentation and therefore lose thrust and power. A refrain runs through a number of the chapters. The services for children are " sadly inadequate " (p 53); for old people " underdeveloped, limited and patchy " (p 90); housing for old people " quite inadequate " (p 92); services for the physically handicapped " in urgent need of development " (p 101); for the chronic sick " seriously inadequate " (p 118); and community care for the mentally disordered " still a sad illusion and judging by published plans will remain so for years ahead " (p 107). Yet the committee failed to bring these indictments together in a major challenge to the Government and public to find massive new resources for the creation of a major new service. Consider the weak advocacy in the introductory pages for a single department and in particular the incomprehensible surrender of judgements about social need to judgements about what is politically expedient in the statement that " it would be naive to think that any massive additional resources will be made available in the near future " (p 15). Even if the committee believed this to be true why did they have to say so and withold an argument which might have won public imagination and induced a readiness to provide more resources?

By failing to document the extent to which services also fell short of needs the committee made it difficult for priorities and the eventual structure of the service to be defined. The nearest it came in fact to specifying requirements on the basis of evidence was in the first few paragraphs of its discussion of services for children. The committee accepted an estimate from appendix Q that " *at least* one child in ten in the population will need special educational, psychiatric or social help before it reaches the age of 18 but that at present *at most* one child in twenty-two is receiving such help " (p 53). This is a deceptively exact statement. What does it mean? The estimate of need includes children who are in poverty, have a whole range of physical handicaps, including asthma and speech defects, are sub-normal and have psychiatric disorders, are in homeless and fatherless families, as well as children who are taken into care and delinquent boys " with at least three court appearances." Quite a variety of trouble. And the reader who attempts to find which needs are least well met will emerge utterly baffled after studying appendix Q. One table includes statistics of the number of children experiencing a condition at a particular time (poverty) and a condition at any time during the first seventeen years of life (admitted to care). There is no discussion of the extent to which the local authority children's service fails to meet need. All that can safely be concluded is that the bulk of unmet needs are those—for special education and training, psychiatric supervision, health services, housing, home help, and financial help—which lie outside the scope of the children's service, as presently administered. But in discussing the new social service department the consequences for its structure and functions are not drawn by the committee.

Yet this matter is crucial if we are to decide what should be the character and function of the future service. If material aid is to be dominant then casework may have to be minimal. If the children's part of the social work services is already reasonably well-developed then the fastest growing parts may be those for the elderly and disabled. This too will be crucial in determining the direction which the new service takes and the kind of staff required. In appendix L the committee lists 90,000 staff working in 1966 in services proposed for inclusion in the new Seebohm department. Only 7,700 of them were child care officers and other social workers. There may be a greater need for a small number of highly trained planners and managerial staff and for a large number of ancillary workers, like home helps and visitors, who receive short spells of training, than for a much larger middle tier of field-workers with a fairly lengthy training.

the resulting aims of the new service

The relationship between research or the collection of evidence and the identification of need is therefore critical. And it is the identification of need on the basis of demonstrable inequality of resources and of degree of social integration that can justify the choice of objectives and the specification of those objectives. It was because the Seebohm Committee did not properly establish needs that it did not properly formulate the aims of the new service. If the reader combs the report he will not find a full and unambiguous statement of the aims of the service. This criticism should not be misunderstood. There are numerous statements about the possible aims of the new service, but these are mostly " second-order " aims. Thus, amalgamation is said to give the service more power to speak up for a rightful share of resources within local administration and help to make the service more adequate (pp 30, 32-33 and 46-47). It is said to break down artificial boundaries between services, reduce divided responsibility and lead to better co-ordination and continuity (pp 31, 34-35 and 44-45). It is said to allow the development of more emphasis on preventive as compared with casualty services for social distress (pp 136-141). A number of specific aims are also expressed in the chapters on particular services.

But perhaps the best general statement about aims is the first paragraph of chapter 7 of the report: " We are convinced that if local authorities are to provide an effective family service they must assume wider responsibilities than they have at present for the prevention, treatment and relief of social problems. The evidence we have received, the visits we have undertaken, and our own experience leave us in no doubt that the resources at present allocated to these tasks are quite inadequate. Much more ought to be done, for example, for the very old and the under fives, for physically and mentally handicapped people in the community, for disturbed adolescents and for the neglected flotsam and jetsam of society. Moreover, the ways in which existing resources are organised and deployed are inefficient. Much more ought to be done in the fields of prevention, community involvement, the guidance of voluntary workers and in making fuller use of voluntary organisations. We believe that the best way of achieving these ends is by setting up a unified social service department which will include the present childrens and welfare services together with some of the social service functions of health, education and housing departments." (p 44).

An impression is given of inchoate, multiple aims and loose reasoning. Is the primary purpose to provide family services for those who lack a family or whose family resources are meagre? If so, there would be profound implications for the organisation of residential homes and hostels for children, the elderly and the mentally and physically handicapped. Either the residential homes would all have to be run on a " family " basis, which is an aim that would require detailed exposition or a policy of closing them down and integrating their occupants in different types of private households would have to be followed. There would be profound implications also for professional social work roles, staffing and training. The system would have to be recast to a very considerable extent.

In opening the debate on the second reading of the Bill in the House of Commons the Secretary of State for Social Services, Mr. Crossman, plainly felt the need for a statement of aims. He said: " The primary objective of the personal social services we can best describe as strengthening the capacity of the family to care for its members and to supply, as it were, the family's place where necessary; that is, to provide as far as may be social support or if necessary a home for people who cannot look after themselves or be adequately looked after in their family. This is not the only objective of the personal social services. They have an important role to play in community development, for example. But it has been the idea of forming a ' family ' service that has inspired the call for a review of the organisation of the services with which the Bill is concerned." (*Hansard*, 26 February 1970, col 1407).

He did not attempt to spell out what this view would imply for the re-organisation of services. Had he attempted to do so; or had the Seebohm Committee done so beforehand, the recommendations would have taken a different form and there might not have been such a friendly welcome to the Bill from all political quarters in Parliament.

For the really important issues have been ducked in securing a precarious consensus. What kind of family relationships should the State support, and in what circumstances? How far must residential institutions be abandoned in favour of true community care? Is professional independence and the opportunity for the expression of public dissent threatened by monolithic bureaucratic conformity? Is the social worker an agent of social control or an articulate representative of minority interests and views? Should community development include a network of information and legal services, a policy of racial integration and an extension of democracy by means of local pressure-groups and protest groups?

a policy for Seebohm departments

A radical statement of objectives would have to start by revealing the extent of inequality of resources and of social isolation and separation. Community development would be seen in terms of the equalisation of resources, the reduction of isolation, family support and community integration. I will describe these briefly in turn.

Although national social services, such as social insurance, family allowances and taxation, would be primarily concerned with the redistribution of resources, local social services have a major part to play in equalising amenities, providing special kinds of housing, supplementing transport services for the elderly and disabled, supplying aids in the home for the handicapped, delivering meals, undertaking housing repairs and improvement, and restocking houses which have become denuded because of debts, drug addiction, alcoholism or a husband's desertion. The identification and mobilisation of resource needs would be a major part of the work of the social worker. The Seebohm department should take the initiative locally in equalising facilities between different sub-areas of the authority and identifying and meeting the special needs of particular communities. For this there must be an area resource plan.

Second, the reduction of isolation. One important means of achieving this is by organising routine visiting services. The Seebohm Committee lamentably failed to understand the importance of these, particularly as a means of prevention and developing comprehensive services. Once routine visiting and assessment is started many sceptics will finally become convinced of the need to expand services. A start could be made with services for people of advanced age, later extending to all the elderly and to the handicapped, including families with handicapped children. One valuable feature of such a service is that social workers would check systematically whether people were receiving the various local and national benefits for which they were eligible. Isolation can also be greatly reduced by means of day clubs and centres, group holidays and improved methods of communication (including telephones). By extension to ethnic groups the same principles can be applied.

Third, support for the family. We have to remind ourselves that any policy aimed at replacing the family is inconceivable in present or prospective conditions. The Seebohm Committee did not consider the evidence that exists of the functions played by the family, and its strengths and shortcomings as a means of obtaining insights into policy. Certainly the " welfare " work of the family for children, the handicapped and the aged, dwarfs that of the officially established social services. And certainly family relationships help to keep people in touch with the feelings and problems of all age-groups, and also help them achieve a sense of individual identity and integrate them with a variety of social groups. Those with slender family resources are those who most commonly receive and need the help of welfare services (see, for example, E. Shanas *et al, Old people in three industrial societies*, chaps 5 and 14, London, Routledge, 1968). Home help services can include shopping, laundry, night attendance, evening relief and accompanied outings, as well as the preparation of meals and domestic cleaning. Several research reports have shown that they need to be expanded rapidly. A recent official survey found that the home help service could be doubled or tripled (Government Social Survey, *The Home Help Service in England & Wales*, London, HMSO, 1970). Adoption and foster-care in approved conditions are extensions of the same principles. Later in this book Michael Meacher, for the elderly, and Peter Mittler, for the mentally handicapped, elaborate this policy.

The aim of supporting the family, however, merges into the fourth aim, that of community integration. Any logical development of a policy of family support must lead to a policy of community as against institutional care. The Seebohm Committee equivocated between the two and did not call attention to the fact, for example, that nearly three times as much is spent by local authorities on residential institutions as on home help services for the elderly and disabled. It also failed to anticipate and resolve a possible conflict between the personnel from children's and welfare departments. The aim of the former has been broadly to keep children with their parents in their own homes and when that cannot be done to place them in foster homes or residential units similar in structure and operation to the family household. I believe that this policy should be applied consistently to handicapped adults and the elderly as well, and that the subjective and objective evidence so far collected supports it. Yet because in the past the local authority welfare department has lacked the means it has practised a rather different policy, of swelling the number of small residential institutions.

The Seebohm Committee recommended that the home help service should be transferred to the new department but did not see the importance of placing the provision and management of sheltered housing under the same auspices. In later chapters of this book John Agate and Hilary Rose also argue that the Seebohm department should have control of sheltered housing. If at the time of admission to residential institutions the handicapped and the elderly (and their relatives) had a genuine choice of either sheltered housing in the community (with home services if necessary) or a residential institution the vast majority would opt for the former and be capable of living there up to the time of requiring admission to hospital.

B

Demand for residential institutions would decline. The new Seebohm departments could not of course start shutting down residential institutions overnight but they could adopt bold but feasible plans giving priority to sheltered housing and home services and gradually reduce residential accommodation. Residential institutions for the elderly and infirm could be transferred by stages to the new area health authorities and placed under the charge of geriatricians and others concerned with the nursing and medical care of those who are incapacitated. This would concentrate the attentions of the new Seebohm-type departments upon community care.

There are other arguments for reducing the emphasis on long-term institutional care, as shown in the anxious discussion going on recently about hospitals for the mentally handicapped. There is evidence in many cases of loss of contacts with relatives and friends without the substitution of social relations with fellow residents. There is the restriction of occupational activity and evidence of loneliness and apathy—by comparison with people of comparable age and physical condition outside. And quite apart from the deplorably low standards of amenities there is also the organisational rigidity of institutional life, which inevitably creates severe problems of adjustment and integration for residents from diverse backgrounds. Many old people are dismayed at the interruption of a life-time's routine, loss of contact with locality and family and reduction of privacy and identity. The closer a residential institution approximates to the scale, privacy and freedom of the private household the greater the qualified expression of contentment. The promise in policy to protect people from admission to institutions except in extreme ill-health could attract public enthusiasm for the new service. In the 1950s and 1960s " community care " has been interpreted variously and because of this is regarded with a measure of cynicism by some students, doctors and social workers. Even the term " community " has no settled meaning in the social sciences (see, for example, M. Stacey, " The myth of community studies," *British Journal of Sociology*, June 1969). But if presented along the lines outlined here, of the equalisation of resources, support of the family, and support for the individual to maintain a private household and an " ordinary " pattern of local relations as opposed to entering a communal institution community care can become a meaningful objective.

Community integration means more, however, than community care. It means the promotion of citizen rights and of certain kinds of group activity. Tony Lynes puts the problem succinctly: " The poor, as such, are in a weak bargaining position. The circumstances which make them poor also tend to make them powerless. Short of violent protest, just how are the homeless and the slum-dwellers, the disabled and the fatherless, to become a force on their own behalf?" (see page 120 below). The Seebohm department can foster this self-assertiveness but only if its relationship with local democracy is carefully worked out, its professional semi-independence of local bureaucracy emphasised and the nature of and training for social work restated. This is a tall order. Perhaps the best chapter in the Seebohm Report is on community development:

" The term 'community development' is used primarily to denote work with neighbourhood groups. Community development in this country is seen as a process whereby local groups are assisted to clarify and express their needs and objectives and to take collective action to attempt to meet them. It emphasises the involvement of the people themselves in determining and meeting their own needs. The role of the community worker is that of a source of information and expertise, a stimulator, a catalyst and an encourager " (p 148).

This view was cautiously presented, however, as adding to existing conceptions of social work rather than replacing them. Extra appointments and experiments were recommended. Certainly the conception of group work is beginning to be worked out in more detail. In 1969 an Association for Groupwork was proposed (M. McNay, *The concept of groupwork in the field of social work,* Association for Groupwork, 21a Kingsland High Street, London E.8). Much can be done in organising tenants' associations, groups of mental hospital outpatients and of drug addicts, the homeless and so on. But group work can only be developed effectively if there are swift improvements in information services, legal services and political machinery.

Local political machinery has not been examined carefully in relation to community development and the evolution of the local social services. The Redcliffe-Maud Commission did not devote very much attention to this question and the opportunity was not taken up in the Government's White Paper on local government reform (Cmnd 4276). There is a haphazard mushrooming of new procedures. The proposals of the Skeffington Report for a community forum and community development officers (*People and Planning,* London, HMSO, 1969) and of the Green Paper on the Health Service need to be linked with the work of the Community Relations Council and Race Relations Board, the Home Office experiments in community development, Ministry of Housing experiments in urban aid and the Seebohm proposals for the participation of the public in the local social services. Much more coherent systems of public involvement in the management of the social services (schools, residential homes, hospitals, day centres and so on), complaints procedures, and accountability of those administering services need to be worked out. At every level the traditional British assumption of the appropriateness of a hierarchial " class " structure needs to be questioned. The consumer should have a much stronger voice in many different and even modest contexts. There is no reason, for example, why old people in residential homes should not have a representative committee which could advise on a diary of events, the menu, the operating rules of management and other relevant matters.

Preventive socialisation

The Seebohm departments should offer information shops in shopping centres. But the main national network of information services should be administered independently of local government. David Bull discusses the potentiality and difficulties of information services in full in a subsequent chapter. While there are a large number of Citizen's Advice Bureaux throughout the country, they are not to be found in many areas and are run on a shoe-string in others.

From aiding and abetting the individual and the family by providing information in a digestible form, it is a logical next step to offer better legal services and to relate the two. In recent years there has been a growth of interest in the social responsibilities of the legal profession (B. Abel-Smith and R. Stevens, *In search of justice*, London, Allen Lane, 1968; Ben Whitaker, *Participation and poverty*, Fabian Research Series 272, 1968; M. Zander, *Lawyers and the public interest*, 1968; Anthony Lester, *Democracy and individual rights*, Fabian Tract 390, 1969). Legal aid for poor families is grossly restricted and is mainly taken up with aid for matrimonial proceedings. There is a strong argument for a two-stage development in information and legal centres. Experimental schemes to increase the amount and quality of legal aid and advice should be financed by the Government and an incentive scheme intrduced to encourage a better distribution of lawyers and persuade more of them to work in poor areas. At a second stage, a National Citizens' Rights Council should be established with members appointed by the Crown on the advice of the Lord Chancellor (R. Brooke, F. Field and P. Townsend, *A policy to establish the legal rights of low income families*, Poverty pamphlet one, Child Poverty Action Group, 1969; and B. Abel-Smith and R. Stevens, *op cit*, p 271). The Government's record in reforming and extending legal services has been dismal and there is as yet little realisation of what can be done to buttress and accelerate community development and the extension of democracy through an expansionist policy for legal and information services. In the meantime the Child Poverty Action Group established in April 1970 an experimental Citizen's Rights Office, including both legal and information services under its director, Mrs. Audrey Harvey. Some other experiments are being tried elsewhere, for example, in Notting Hill, London. (*Freedom and choice: a community planning project for Notting Hill*, Notting Hill Housing Service and Research Group, June 1969). Inevitably such experimental offices will need to have very close relations with the new Seebohm departments, and can do much to offer short courses of training in welfare rights to social workers.

The repercussions for the type of work undertaken by Seebohm-type departments would be considerable. There would be greater stress on the provision of information, the exploration and notification of need for financial, material and domestic aid, the initiation of contacts between families in need and appropriate pressure-groups as well as appropriate social and occupational groups, and, finally, representation of the needs and problems of families to authority—housing and education departments, supplementary benefit offices, the new lower tier local councils proposed by the Redcliffe-Maud Commission and the district committees proposed by the Green Paper on the Health Services, as well as the new main councils and the central departments of government. All this demands a large measure of professional autonomy on the part of senior staff. It also has ramifications for the training and ideology of social workers and these questions are discussed at length in this book by Adrian Sinfield.

What is at stake is the quality of family and community life and the whole direction of community development. Is the new Seebohm service to be a poorly financed, meagre department which takes the edge off the distress and deprivation arising in modern society and which, in effect, reinforces the assumptions of an increasingly inegalitarian society? Or is it to be the fifth major social service, of a scale equivalent, eventually, in manpower and expenditure to the health, education, housing and social security services which has a deliberate commitment to the reduction of inequalities of resources and of social isolation, whether of individuals or groups?

A force for conformity to hierarchial society, or a force for non-conformity in an equal one?

summary

This book is about the quality of local community. The Seebohm Committee did not undertake the research or adequately assess the evidence that is available so as to establish community needs. As a consequence it did not express clearly the objectives of the service, its priorities and its future organisation, structure and functions. The case for doubling or tripling material and domestic services, implementing a systematic system of community as compared with institutional or residential care (for example, by rapid development of visiting services and sheltered housing) and for involving the community more effectively in the management of services was not made, or not made forcefully. Although the Committee recommended a variety of reforms, the one given greatest attention was expressed in terms of administrative unification of local social services or a tidying-up operation believed to pave the way for greater co-ordination of service. Conflicting elements in the proposed department—such as casework and groupwork, material aid and advisory services, and differences of aim between children's and welfare officers— were not identified or raised for discussion.

However, the problems which might arise as a consequence of extending the power of officials over a larger area, creating a monopoly of certain kinds of service, weakening some citizens' power to seek redress for maladministration and neglect through alternative organisations, and emphasising the professional power of social work, were not examined critically enough. With minor changes, except for a failure to provide for effective central direction, the Government has incorporated the main recommendations in the Local Authority Social Services Bill.

In short, a great opportunity has been missed. It is an opportunity to launch a major new Family or Community Welfare Service (for that would be a more accurate term), together with a dramatic extension of information and legal services in a (costly) programme of community development. Such a programme is badly needed. The isolation and deprivation of the elderly and disabled, the poverty of environment of some local authority areas, such as their lack of play facilities, the difficulties in adversity of ordinary families with children, the problems of looking after elderly and handicapped dependants and the fear of losing one's home and having to enter an institution, are problems which are widely recognised and should be of central concern to the new service. They are seen to diminish the quality of life itself. The formal aims of a programme of community development, which arise from an analysis of different kinds of inequality should be fourfold: the equalisation of resources locally; the reduction of isolation; family support and community integration. These aims have been outlined briefly to show how they could be related in a coherent plan. They are the meat and drink of socialism.

2. which way for social work?

Adrian Sinfield

A social service department, providing a community based and family oriented service available to all—this was the major recommendation of the Seebohm Committee on *Local authority and allied personal social services* (cmnd 3703). This new department will have responsibilities extending well beyond those of existing local authority departments and will, the Committee stated, " reach far beyond the discovery and rescue of social casualties; it will enable the greatest possible number of individuals to act reciprocally, giving and receiving service for the well-being of the whole community " (para 2).

But far-ranging as the report was, it provided little answer to the basic issues facing the social work profession and the planner of the social services in this country to-day. What contributions has the profession to make in our efforts to improve the quality of life in a modern industrial society? What are the priorities for social workers—whom should they be helping and how? How do we ensure that the services of social workers are " available for all?" And how do we maintain the quality of these services?

These issues stand for any profession, whatever type or form of co-ordination is eventually implemented. They were in fact posed some eighteen years ago by Richard Titmuss in his inaugural lecture as the first professor of social administration in the University of London, when he spoke of the problem of priorities. " In a situation of limited resources, quality of service comes into conflict with quantity of service." " To what extent, if at all," he asked " are contemporary social needs being artificially developed by the professional, administrative and technical interests upon whose skills the services depend? What, to put it crudely, are we getting for our money? Is an increasing proportion of the cost going, first, to those who do the welfare rather than to those who need the welfare and second, for treating at a higher standard the symptoms of need rather than in curing or preventing the causes of need?" (reprinted in *Essays on "the welfare state,"* pp 23-24, Allen and Unwin, 1958).

unification and social work professionalisation

These questions gain added importance in the light of the Seebohm recommendations for the unification of the social services which will increase the professionalisation of social work. Both unification and increased professionalisation may bring considerable advantages. The firm establishment of a profession may lead to the strengthening of the professional in defence of his client, to higher quality in work and a greater assumption of responsibilities. But, equally professionalisation may bring dangers, coming between the worker and his client or the community at large.

Unification may serve a multitude of purposes. It may lead to a saving of resources and reduplication of work, to a greater degree of consultation, and so collaboration in the provision of services, and to a better service to the public. It may strengthen the professional against the bureaucrat, but also against the public, and may help to legitimise demands for further privileges, rights and benefits to be awarded in deference to assured professional status.

There is the danger of " rigor professionis " if the co-ordinated units are set up too quickly. The social work profession may unify and very largely withdraw into itself. It may continue to refine and develop its existing skills but neglect its responsibility to adjust to the changing needs and expectations of the people and the community it exists to serve. There is the danger too that current disillusion with, and opposition towards, bureaucracies, and officialdom—the whole structure of establishment—may lead to an increase in the ever-present tension between the community and its official caretakers. As a result the larger departments may simply become even more isolated than the existing ones while " grass-roots " organisations multiply to help small areas and groups but without the power or the permanence to achieve more than a holding operation.

It is vital that these dangers should be faced now and discussed widely inside and outside the profession. An anonymous commentator has written " For those of us who have been looking forward to an authoritative case being made for the establishment of a comprehensive social work service, the Seebohm Committee has served us well " (anon Case Conference, August 1968, p 140). A citizen reading the report might indeed conclude that it had more to do with the work satisfaction and career structure of the professional social worker than it had to do with his own needs or rights in the modern welfare state.

Ten years ago Barbara Wootton referred to social workers as " largely the victims of the contemporary obsession with professionalism . . . the second revolution of the past half-century . . . One of the more regrettable features of the Younghusband Report is the unqualified and undiscriminating blessing which it gives to this " (" Daddy Knows Best," Twentieth Century, Winter 1959, p 256). There is a danger that the Seebohm report may have made the same mistake.

The Report received a generally enthusiastic reception at its publication in July 1968. " A great State paper " was the description by David Donnison, Professor of Social Administration in the University of London, in an article in the special enlarged October issue of Social Work. " For many social workers," the editorial declared, it represented " the fulfilment of their highest hopes." One of the leading members of the Seebohm Committee described it as the most important report for social work since " the Majority Report of the Royal Commission on the Poor Laws " in 1909 (the report signed by Charles Loch of the Charity Organisation

Society, not the Minority Report signed by George Lansbury and Beatrice Webb). In the debate in the House of Lords lavish praise was bestowed on the committee which had produced a "black and white report" with "more than 200 specific recommendations," and the report was constantly coupled with that of Beveridge in 1942 as one of the landmarks in British social policy (House of Lords, 29 January 1969, cols 1168-1193 and 1198-1274).

Only a few voices have been raised in opposition, the most critical being a perhaps prudently anonymous medical officer who regarded it as "a national disaster." Yet while some social workers have described it as revolutionary, others have argued that it is only a tidying-up or "an enabling instrument for further work to be done."

This last view is perhaps the most accurate. After all the committee's terms of reference were "to review the organisation and responsibilities of the local authority personal social services in England and Wales, and to consider what changes are desirable to secure an effective family service" (para 1). Although refusing to be shackled by these terms on many issues, the committee did not reach any clearly-stated conclusion as to what constituted "an effective family service." This phrase reappears throughout the seven hundred paragraphs of the Report but there is little clarification of what is really meant. Ironically there is no chapter on the needs of the family and its social services but only ones on categories of children, old people, physically handicapped people and mentally subnormal and mentally ill people. The clearest reference indicates not the sort of service provided or need met but "a service which is accessible and acceptable and which meets the need promptly, that is, a service which is as far as possible community based" (para 582).

the urgent but unmet need for basic research

To provide this "effective family service" which will be "available for all" it is clearly necessary to have information about the basic needs which such a service will have to meet. It is also essential to know what needs are currently being met, and in what way, and to know in detail the ways in which current services are failing.

Ten years ago the last major report on social work prior to Seebohm, the Young-husband report, firmly and clearly called for basic research. "We were struck, in planning the field inquiries, by the lack of any systematic study of the part played by social workers in meeting needs within the framework of the social services. Such information could have had an important bearing on our own inquiry. We should like to draw attention to the desirability of such a study. We think much of the confusion in regard to the functions of social workers in the health and welfare services, as elsewhere, is due to lack of analyses of this kind " (*Report of the working party on social workers in the local authority health and welfare services,* Ministry of Health, Department of Health for Scotland, 1959, para 11, see also paras 26 and 563). In fact the chairman of this committee had been stressing the need for such research for many years.

What could be clearer and more precise? Yet ten years later very little has been done to remedy this basic defect. The confusion referred to in the Younghusband report may derive not only from a lack of analyses but also, at least in part, from an actual confusion in the functions of the social workers. Seebohm and his committee do not clarify this, let alone attempt to fill the gap in our knowledge of the basic operations of the existing system. Indeed, one of the most remarkable aspects of their whole report is its lightning tour of the deficiencies of the existing system as if the case were already proven and documented elsewhere. In just twenty-eight paragraphs in five pages we are given an astonishingly brief and undetailed account. There are, we are told, deficiencies in the amount, range and quality of provision. These three failings are exacerbated by poor co-ordination, by the difficulty of access for the would-be consumer and others such as doctors, and by insufficient adaptability to meet changes in the nature and extent of social need. Equally briefly, within these same twenty-eight paragraphs, we are presented with the " underlying causes of these shortcomings." These are, apparently, lack of sufficient resources, lack of knowledge (though on this we are invited to see further in chapter XV) and divided responsibility (paras 73-100).

Still, Seebohm too adds strong support to the demand for research (chapter XV). Lack of it " makes no sense in terms of administrative efficiency, and, however little intended, it indicates a *careless* attitude towards human welfare." (para 455, emphasis added). This in fact is an indictment of current practice. Very little opportunity has been taken of the great amount of encouragement in legislation for agencies to undertake research. For example under the Children's and Young Persons' Act of 1963 the Home Secretary and local authority children's departments have power to carry out, or to assist others in undertaking, research into child care and adoption and the statutory Advisory Council on Child Care established in 1948 has recommended five areas as a guide to research. The Health Visitors and Social Work Training Act of 1962 also encouraged research but as yet there has been little, if any, visible result of these invitations having been taken up.

While many social workers clearly have reservations about the value of research, Seebohm and his committee did not. " We cannot emphasise too strongly the part which research must play in the creation and maintenance of an effective family service. Social planning is an illusion without adequate facts; and the adequacy of services mere speculation without evaluation . . . It must be a continuing process, accepted as a permanent and familiar feature of any department or agency concerned with social provision." (para 473).

"daddy should know better by now"

However much reports emphasize the essential need for research and social work textbooks stress the importance of client self-determination, there has been very little energy devoted to finding out what the recipients of social workers' help think of the services. Both the Younghusband and Seebohm reports, nine years apart, give similar and unconvincing reasons for not doing consumer research. " We should like to have undertaken a complementary inquiry into the reactions of those using the services. An investigation of this nature would, however, have prolonged our own inquiries unduly " (Younghusband, para 10). Appointed in June 1955, the working party reported in February 1959. The Seebohm Committee sat for some two and a half years and reflected in 1968 " We were, regrettably, unable to sound consumer reaction to the services in any systematic fashion. This was also related to the fact that we made no attempt to organise a research programme as this would have delayed publication perhaps for another year or two " (para 43).

Given the increasing emphasis on democratic participation and the fact that it was appointed by a socialist government, Seebohm's disregard for the potential or past customer of the social services is the more disturbing. Perhaps it is even more remarkable, or ironic, or just revealing, that the committee set up to assess the most appropriate training for community work, and chaired by Dame Eileen Younghusband, not only undertook no consumer research (perhaps because it was thought to be too expensive) but also made no reference to the lack of such enquiries—as if indeed they were of no relevance. The committee itself consisted strictly of " experts "—teachers or administrators in the social services and community work (*Community work and social change*, pp XI-XIII, Longmans). This persistent neglect of the recipient, let alone the potential recipient of social workers' services, is particularly surprising, and disappointing, given the emphatic and astringent criticism of the Younghusband Report by Barbara Wootton in 1959. " Everything is viewed from the administrative angle, through administrative spectacles—benevolently, no doubt, but always from outside, at second hand. Only those who supply the various services, never those for whose benefit they are supplied, are fit to judge their quality. Be quiet, dear, Daddy knows best." (*op cit*).

THE EFFICACY OF SOCIAL WORK

Implicit in much that is said about the services provided by social workers seems to be the assumption that anything is better than nothing. This is linked to the fact that, because most social workers feel themselves overworked, they do not very often stop to consider what their work is achieving nor whether it should be redirected And because they are overburdened, they have little opportunity to follow the experiences of their clients; and they seem even less likely to do this when responsibilities cross jurisdictional boundaries. As the American poet Robert Frost said " It couldn't be called ungentle, but how thoroughly departmental." Though of course, we hope that co-ordination will at least put a stop to this fragmentation of responsibility.

The Seebohm report never appears to question the efficacy of social work. Yet this question cannot be ignored if we are to decide whether the Seebohm proposals are adequate. This crucial issue has received scarcely any attention from the social work profession, though without a clear and positive answer the necessity for social workers, and more of them, must remain largely a matter of faith.

In 1959 Mr. Robin Huws Jones asked " is our social worker really necessary?" and answered himself in the fourth of his twenty-nine paragraphs " surely only a modern Voltaire could deny that he sees the necessity!" (*The Almoner*, vol 12, no 2, p 61). Mr. Huws Jones however does go on to talk about the effectiveness of social work of all types, admitting the need to define the aims of " social work in specific, realistic operational terms " (*ibid* p 67, and see also D. E. G. Plowman, " What are the outcomes of social work?", *Social Work* (GB), January 1969). Mr. Huws Jones believes that much help could be provided by the social sciences but confesses to " a disloyal spasm of sympathy with the complaint that the sociologists' cry is ' Give us the job and we'll spend the next seven years sharpening the tools'." This is a fair complaint about my own profession but it is doubtful whether many sociologists in this country have been approached for help. And this certainly does not explain the virtual failure of the social work profession to get on with its own research. Certainly some projects have been started since the Younghusband report but mostly on a very small scale. At the University of York a survey is just starting on the roll of medical social workers and the National Institute of Social Work Training has undertaken a potentially most valuable study evaluating social work help for a sample of 300 people aged 70 and over who receive welfare services in a London borough.

" girls at vocational high "

In the United States there have been more attempts to evaluate social work and measure its effectiveness. The best known is probably *Girls at vocational high,* an examination of the effect of social work counselling on some 200 teenage girls with a control sample of the same size. I shall describe this study in a little detail because it seems to illustrate some of the basic problems facing social work in all countries. The very cautious conclusion of the book was that " on these (objective) tests no strong indications of effect (of counselling) are found and the conclusion must be stated in the negative when it is asked whether social work intervention with potential problem high school girls was in this instance effective." (H. J. Meyer *et al*, *Girls at vocational high*, p180, Russell Sage, New York, 1958). There was a marked discrepancy between the results of the objective tests of progress and the subjective evaluation of the social workers involved: this led the investigators to compare the workers' evaluation with the familiar " the operation was a success but the patient died." The social workers in fact tended to pay more attention to the ways in which the girls actually behaved during their counselling sessions rather than to the effect of the counselling on behaviour outside these sessions (*ibid* p 157). This is a danger of the psycho-therapeutic process when the social worker may become so engrossed in building up a relationship that he may lose sight of his reason for doing it.

Many criticisms can be, and some have been, made of the study both in its methodology and its theoretical analysis (see for the defence of the social workers, M. E. MacDonald, " Reunion at vocational high," *Social service review*, June 1966). Of course, too sweeping claims have been made for its findings which have been extended to cover—and denounce—the whole of social work. The blame here must lie not just with the publicists but with a profession that has persistently failed to evaluate its own efficacy. This failure to validate techniques can be partly explained, I think, by the fact that many social workers have come to regard themselves as checking their own work in the process of casework counselling itself and in the course of discussion with colleagues and supervisors. The criteria for " success " therefore are their own and not their clients'. For many the journey—the casework or group session—has almost certainly become the goal. Clients who are unwilling to discuss their difficulties in this way are classified as " unco-operative " or " lacking in insight." Some talk of a client's " willingness to use the casework relationship " or his " ability to use the service." In the last resort then it may be seen as the client who is the failure.

The social worker's own insights into the individual's problems may often be determined by the techniques employed. *Girls at vocational high* revealed very clearly that the use of different social work techniques led the social worker to change *her* view of the client's situation, and so brought her to consider different ways of solving the client's problem. In individual casework the social worker was more likely to assume that a client was magnifying or distorting the problem in some way. In group sessions the worker was compelled to recognise that what the client said was true, as in these sessions the girls had a greater opportunity to " bring in their world." " When all or a majority of members of the group, in spite of differences in their psychological make-up, almost simultaneously described situations of external stress in similar ways, the worker herself came to view the problem differently . . . Discussions of violent acts — suicide, gang warfare — occurred frequently in the group sessions. However in the group setting it seemed clear to the leaders that talk about such things was more related to actual happenings than to the girls' inner preoccupations with such events." (*ibid* pp 133-34). In some ways the authors come close to reversing the conventional wisdom of "treating" the deep-seated internal causes and argue for treating what is often called the "presenting problem." They argued that social workers needed to pay much greater attention to possible environmental changes in helping their clients. "Should we expect weekly interviews with caseworkers," the authors ask, "or weekly counselling sessions in groups, to have critical effects when situational conditions were hardly touched?" (p 214). They lay stress on the importance for the social work profession of developing means of bringing about changes in the social conditions rather than trying to help clients by "indirect efforts through influences on internal psychological states." Helping a girl to stay on and get through school with material assistance is given low priority by the social workers in the study but failure to achieve this may make other desirable objectives even less attainable. Altogether this study emphasises the need not to let casework roles get out of proportion and the need to attempt new, and as yet less professionally fashionable, methods of help.

the definition of social work

It is impossible to study the effectiveness of social work, however, without inviting a clearer definition of social work. One definition of *case*work, provided by the Younghusband report (para 638), is "a personal service provided by qualified workers for individuals who require skilled assistance in resolving some material, emotional or character problem." Such an all-inclusive definition led Barbara Wootton to comment "if these skills really exist, surely they are wasted upon obscure members of the British working-class: would not the caseworkers do better to get their hands on some of our world's rulers?" (*op cit*, p 253).

As recently as 1968 in a textbook on concepts the *aim of* casework was said to be "to help the client to manage in the community either simply with the aid of encouragement from the caseworker or also by changing some of the client's attitudes if they are proving harmful" (Jonathan Moffet, *Concept in casework treatment*, pp 3-4, Routledge and Kegan Paul, 1968). This would seem to plunge us back into the social and economic vacuum of the client-worker relationship, a view which I am often told has been abandoned by social workers. Although it may have been by the practitioners, it certainly does not appear to have been rejected by many of those responsible for training the new social workers.

The difficulty of explaining and defining the skills peculiar to casework is well illustrated in a study of medical social workers' attachment to a group practice. " I have tried to discount any suggestion that casework is a mysterious skill only to be practised by an elite," writes the medical social worker, yet concludes the same sentence " but I should like to be equally emphatic that practising without a sound knowledge of human behaviour is *wrong and dangerous.*" (J. A. S. Forman and E. M. Fairbairn, *Social Casework in General Practice,* p 79, Oxford University Press, 1968, emphasis added). " This knowledge," the writer adds, " may not be gained in a quick or superficial way."

But within two pages of this forthright declaration Miss Fairbairn ends the chapter " *Casework is commonsense*—casework is having the imagination to foresee what might go wrong in a plan for an old lady's discharge and preparing for it in advance —casework is feeling sufficiently involved to accept the work and carry the responsibility." (*ibid,* p 81, emphasis added again).

To illustrate the difficulties involved I have deliberately quoted from a study that is highly regarded by many social workers. It illustrates the dilemma that faces social workers who wish to claim possession of a special body of knowledge and appropriate techniques. Some would then want to claim a monopoly of these skills and to demand that only the fully qualified should be allowed to practise, and would concentrate their energy on refining these techniques with the hope that social work might be recognised as a science. It was this part of the profession, mainly teachers, whom Barbara Wootton so vigorously attacked in chapter IX of *Social science and social pathology,* (Allen & Unwin, 1959).

Although I believe this group is currently declining in strength—and has never been so influential in Britain as in the United States—their concern has tended to direct the questions that the profession has been asking inward into its own processes and led it to neglect the client.

SOCIAL WORK AND SOCIETY

Social work might better be understood in social terms and not only sociopsychological terms. A social worker imparts information about rights, makes services available, helps to communicate needs to those in authority, and encourages action by the individual, family and group on their own behalf as well as on the behalf of the community. The advantage of this definition is that it suggests the role the social worker can play in the community whatever type of social work or organisational attachment.

This moves the emphasis away from the skills and techniques used and towards the objectives of the worker. In fact, although the social worker is trained to make contact with his "client," studies such as *Girls at vocational high* show how his understanding has been limited by his skills. As Forder says in his new edition of *Penelope Hall's Social Services of Modern England,* "information about the social services has been poorly disseminated; the social and psychological barriers that prevent people from using them have been ignored; professional workers have often been more concerned to have 'co-operative' clients on whom to practise their skills, than to draw their clients into active participation in the aims of the service; those who have been unable to make effective use of the service have been too readily labelled 'unco-operative' and rejected on this basis. Criticisms of the services by the consumers, even constructive criticism, is not generally encouraged and usually resented." (p 294, Routledge and Kegan Paul, 1969).

blowing in the wind

How far does the current narrow interpretation of this role and the lack of facilities and the inadequate services and resources available to him, leave the social worker with an acute sense of helplessness? This is a question that many social workers are greatly concerned about but so far there has been little attempt to bring this to the notice of a wider audience. With the exception of often rather oblique comments in chapter XIII on housing, the Seebohm committee scarcely raised this issue.

Indeed many social workers do see themselves as faced with the task of persuading people to tolerate the intolerable. They become agents of control or "social tranquilisers" (The Social Workers' Group of the Socialist Medical Association, *A socialist view of social work,* p 13, no date). Despite their frustration most stay on in the hope of making the best of a bad job. Their dissatisfaction however is often evidenced by the vigorous support given by many social workers to such organisations as the Child Poverty Action Group and the Disablement Income Group, both established in 1965.

At the same time, there are many social workers who disapprove of such activities and some senior workers in children's departments have regarded attempts by younger colleagues to obtain written explanations of supplementary benefit assessments as "militant." (Child Poverty Action Group, *Poverty,* no 5, p 2, Winter 1967).

Some social workers whom I met in the last few months did not even know of either of these groups and had no idea what was meant by for example the "wage stop," (the procedure whereby supplementary benefit—formerly national assistance—is not paid above the level that a man, unemployed or temporarily sick, is expected to receive in net wages even if his entitlement, because of a high rent, large family or some special need, is higher than this. Some 28,000 families headed by an unemployed man alone had their allowances reduced for this reason in February 1969.

social workers and the attack on inequalities

In examining the role of social work in a modern industrial and still class-bound society, it is vital to analyse its relevance to the basic issues of inequality and privilege. It is still widely believed that the social services, as the other parts of the " welfare state," are instruments of redistribution reducing inequality. A typical and recent statement of this view was made by T. H. Marshall, formerly professor of sociology and Head of the Social Science Department at the London School of Economics. " The social services proper—in health, welfare, education, housing, etc.—have undoubtedly had a profound effect on the distribution of *real* income " (*Political Quarterly*, Jan-March 1969, pp 6-7, emphasis in the original). This seems clear and categorical enough, but a few sentences later Marshall changes his position remarkably. " This has been their aim . . . it is hard to say how much progress has been made."

No doubt they are redistributive, as are any other allocation of services or resources in kind. The important question is not " Do they redistribute?" but the much more complicated set of questions " In what directions do the social services distribute and redistribute? To what extent? How? and for how long, and with what effect?" The answers to these questions then need to be set against the intentions in policy as to the extent and direction of redistribution. The Seebohm Committee disregarded these questions in deciding what constituted an " effective family service."

Yet it is vital to know the actual effect of social workers in distributing resources in kind in a society which is still more or less rigidly stratified by class and where there has been no significant downward redistribution of earnings since the beginning of this century. As long ago as the census of 1911 the proportion of average earnings received by unskilled and semi-skilled working men was the same as it was in 1960—about 79 per cent and 86 per cent respectively. (Guy Routh, *Occupation and pay in Great Britain* 1906-1960, p 107, Cambridge University Press, 1965).

There have been fluctuations since 1911 but two world wars, a cold war, the depression of the 1920s and 1930s and the introduction of the social welfare legislation after 1945 has not lessened occupational differentials at all between the main groups. In 1911 the average unskilled man's wage was 31 per cent of the average manager's, by 1960 this had fallen slightly to 29 per cent. If one considers that in the 1911 census, aeroplane pilots and aviators were grouped with acrobats, magicians and conjurers in the same occupational category headed " performer, showman," one has some idea of the vast changes that have occurred over this period. These have nevertheless done very little to alter the differences between the main groups in the socio-economic structure of Britain.

In 1955 Richard Titmuss questioned the extent of redistribution by government and the reduction of inequalities by all forms of social services in " The social division of welfare " (*op cit*). In the last ten years an increasing amount of evidence has been published revealing that the total resources of many are well below the average standard of living. In 1960 as many as one in eight households existed at a level no better than that of the recipients of national assistance. (B. Abel-Smith and P. Townsend, *The poor and the poorest*, Bell, 1965, and for a summary of research into poverty, A. Sinfield, " Poverty rediscovered," *Race*, October 1968).

The apparent lack of interest on the part of social workers in the command of resources—or at least the vocal or literary members of the profession—must be related to two facts. Until very recently few were aware of the persistent inequalities in the distribution of resources and opportunities that survived the introduction of the " welfare state " and even today many social workers seem to see little relevance in the problems of inequality or the stratified class structure within which they are working. They do not pay sufficient heed to the possible connections between simple lack of resources and personal and family " disintegration."

Secondly, many social workers and social administrators have consciously striven to escape the image of charity workers amongst the poor, and some seem to have believed that in this way they could best improve the standing of their own discipline. They have welcomed the " welfare state," worried about the effects of over-dependency resulting from its " feather-bedding," and departed to fields of research and practice more in touch with the " better classes." The poverty they did see they tended to dismiss as due to the *misuse*, rather than the *lack*, of resources. Indeed, it can be argued that the emphasis on psychodynamic techniques in social work in the 1950s did much to make the poor " silent " or " invisible."

The chairman of the Seebohm committee however estimated that poverty and bad housing " probably cause something like 60 per cent of the work that is now carried on by social workers." (in a broadcast *Dole with everything*, Radio 4, 23 January 1969). Now this sort of statement backed up by evidence could be of great help in establishing the priorities for action for the social services. It also supports very strongly the view that much social work activity is simply a holding operation. If the energies of social workers are directed more towards the poor, there are strong grounds for thinking this leads more to social control than to social welfare and any redistribution of resources. It is a pity that there is no such comment, or evidence for it, in the Seebohm report. Given a different emphasis and a greater concern with material and environmental causes of family breakdown and individual frustration, the profession of social work might well have played a leading role in making society aware much earlier of the persistence of poverty. Instead, the major social work discovery of the 1950s was the " problem family " with an emphasis on the problems that came from within. It was left to others to pursue the questions of the level of social security payments and of individual rights.

the unfathomed extent of needs

Although the Seebohm committee seem to have been concerned about the lack of co-ordination leading to *multiple* visiting as much as that leading to *no* visiting and needs remaining unknown, it did however recognise the great extent of unmet needs and stressed how little was known about those who required help but did not seek or receive it. In an appendix to the report, J. Packman and M. Power estimate that "there are at least as many children in need of help as there are receiving help" (appendix Q, p 354).

The extent to which old people need the most basic help, let alone that of highly-trained and highly-paid workers, and did not receive it was made clear by a cross-national study of old people in three industrial societies, Britain, Denmark and the United States. Of those who were " unable to bathe themselves even with difficulty " 37 per cent received no help at all and only 7 per cent were helped by the social services in Britain. In Denmark the proportion without any help was 5 per cent and in the United States 4 per cent. While by many other criteria British provision was as high as, or even greater than, that of the other two countries, the extent of unmet need was still great. Four per cent of those who had difficulty in preparing meals received help from the social services while eleven per cent had no help at all. Although one per cent received " meals on wheels," six times as many seemed to be in need of them. Even then most recipients had meals only on one or two days a week. (P. Townsend in E. Shanas et al, *Old people in three industrial societies*, Routledge and Kegan Paul, 1968).

Smaller surveys also document the unmet need, especially among the very poor. In a study of large families in London, eleven of the eighteen families with an income below the then national assistance level reported that they rarely saw a health visitor, school care committee worker or any other " lady from the welfare." They did not mention any of them, either, as people they would get in touch with when in difficulty. (Hilary Land, *Large families in London*, Bell, 1970). The government's own study of fifty-one families wage-stopped on assistance, Dennis Marsden's of fatherless families on assistance and the present writer's of unemployed on Tyneside also found very few poor families in contact with any of the social services. In that survey I questioned all families about the services they contacted or that contacted them but abandoned this because of a very high "nil" response and because of my own needs to shorten the questionnaire. At the time (1963-64) I had assumed that this type of research was being carried out more carefully elsewhere, so gave low priority to a tangential aspect of my own research and did not document systematically any of the data. But such research does not seem to have been undertaken.

the client's perspective

The few studies of social workers on the job that have been made have depended basically upon the worker's records or account. The reality of such reports appears to be accepted without question and the worker's view of the client regarded as final. The one-sidedness of these accounts deserves emphasis: it is all too easy to forget, when relationships are unequal, that the account of the person closest to the researcher or reader may not be the only version. (It is worth noting that this inequality is reflected in the convention of adding " was said to have stated " when quoting a " client " recalling a social worker's remarks but not when a social worker reports a client).

One small study of fifteen dissatisfied working-class clients shows the client and the social worker in a Kafka-esque situation, each expecting different reactions of the other. Consulting a social worker about the behaviour of a third party (usually a spouse or a child) clients were disconcerted to find that the social worker took no sides and gave no advice; he simply asked questions and then suggested a further meeting. They were particularly taken aback because most of the questions were directed to the client and *his* feelings and expectations rather than to the behaviour of the third party (J. E. Mayer and N. Timms, " Clash in perspective between worker and client," *Social Casework* (USA) January 1969. This is part of a larger study of sixty-one clients of the London Family Welfare Association, *The client speaks: working class impressions of casework*, Routledge and Kegan Paul, London, forthcoming). Mayer and Timms seem to see the causes of this disjunction in the different cultural systems of the working-class client and the apparently middle-class social worker, each having a different mode of problem-solving. But is the difficulty primarily a difference of culture? If the worker had some knowledge of this, could he bridge the gap between himself and his client? From my own experience of interviewing recipients of the social services I am inclined to attach more significance to the inequality of the relationship and to the very different positions in the socio-economic structure of the social worker and his working-class client. In addition Mayer and Timms tend to overlook the fact that the client often urgently wants help to escape from the immediate crisis.

In 1963-64 I interviewed unemployed families on Tyneside and a year later in

Syracuse, New York State. In both areas I came across many instances of what one might call " sweated social workers " with enormous caseloads, reserves of endurance, and incredible resourcefulness. At the same time I slowly became aware of the ways in which much of the social worker-client contact diverged from the textbook picture and from sociologists' view of the server-client relationship (see for example Goffman, *Asylums*, pp 321 *et seq*, Doubleday Anchor, New York, 1961). Although in many respects the picture that emerged was the same in the two areas in the two countries, the comments that follow apply to the families', and my, experiences with workers in the children's, health and welfare departments of one local authority and the local hospitals. Occasional contact with local authority departments in other parts of Britain suggests that my findings might apply more widely; and this belief has been supported by many social workers.

Both the unemployed and I were made aware of the various minor indignities inflicted on applicants for services, the coldness and sometimes deliberate rudeness of social workers—deliberate in that it was explained to me, confidentially afterwards, that it did a man good to be "dressed down" in front of a room full of people and to be questioned about his search for work. (This was not the local authority social worker's responsibility: besides, the man was disabled and unskilled and only unemployed three months, at a time when many absolutely fit unskilled labourers had been workless for six months). What surprised me most, I think, was the number of times families seemed to be treated discourteously by social workers. There was often no apology for keeping a woman waiting for an hour or more, or for having one's cup of tea in front of clients without offering them one. Sitting at a desk and busy with papers, some social workers did not look up when the client entered or welcome him in and one began the interview, still without looking at the client, " All right, sit down Mrs. ———. Now what is it this time?" At the very least such lack of good manners affected the establishment of a relationship.

People in fact often commented on this to me. I began to get the impression that they experienced peremptory treatment more often from the professionally-qualified social worker, teacher or doctor than they did from local or central government officials. It may have been that the clients were particularly sensitive to this because they felt on a less equal footing with the professional. But there did seem to be little attempt to explain to a family what was being done with them in a way that they understood. All these points seem to be ones of what Miss Fairbairn would call " commonsense " and would appear essential for achieving social work objectives. As Noel Timms has pointed out, although social work " activity has been described as the attempt to cure through talk," . . . " language does not occupy a central place in social work and social workers themselves appear indifferent to its significance." (*Language of social casework*, pp 1-2, Routledge and Kegan Paul).

When he was interviewing fatherless families on assistance in two towns in 1965-66, Dennis Marsden asked them about the help that they received from social services. Most seemed to have had little knowledge of where they could have gone for help and others were often dissatisfied with the advice they received. One separated wife whose husband was mentally ill and alcoholic went to a Citizen's Advice Bureau and was told " ' Men are funny things you know. You've got to give in to them, you've got to humour them.' ' You can go back to him ' she said ' I'm not so fussed for a man as you are.' " Of course, this was a voluntary worker who had only received a very brief preliminary training but it should be pointed out that the customer will not necessarily be aware of this — or regard it as a sufficient explanation. Besides one must face the fact that only a small proportion of all social workers are trained. A probation officer told one woman " Oh, I've got far more important things to do than listen to marriage arguments " (D. Marsden, *Mothers alone: fatherless families in poverty*, Allen Lane Press, Penguin).

Maybe these accounts were exaggerations. Indeed it is very tempting to dismiss all such remarks for one reason or another and very easy—perhaps too easy— to present convincing psychological grounds to explain apparent resentment of help given. What we need to know in undertaking a re-ordering of existing programmes is how representative and accurate these accounts are. There are admittedly two sides to what happens in any encounter. But the client's recollection and definition of the situation is important in determining both the effectiveness of services and the extent to which she is likely to make further use of them, or recommend others to do so.

In both studies the low status of those applying for advice or help seemed very relevant to the treatment they received. Perry Levinson has also emphasised the importance of the inequality in the relationship between the social worker and his clients. It is important, he argues, to study not just the relationship between two people, but between two people occupying often very different positions in the social structure, and meeting in a social organisation which has certain specific powers and which expects certain sorts of behaviour from those to whom it provides help. (*Chronic dependency: a conceptual analysis*, US Department of Health, 1964).

MANPOWER AVAILABILITY

Clearly any reorganisation of the social workers' services must take into account the manpower available, its level of qualification and its distribution across the country.

According to the Seebohm committee's definition of social workers, there were over 11,000 social workers in 1967 employed in the local authority services for children, mental health and welfare, the probation service and the hospital services. Nearly two in five were professionally qualified but the same proportion of practising social workers in those agencies had neither a qualification nor a declaration of recognition of experience. The estimate of one in two trained by 1975 looked optimistic at the best of times: after the cuts in central and local government expenditure it looks even less likely.

The proportion of these workers with professional qualifications was highest in the probation service (69 per cent) and the hospital services (62 per cent). About a third were professionally qualified among full-time field officers in the children's department and among senior officers in the mental health services. For the rest the proportion was lower than one in five and only one in ten of non-senior social workers in the local authority welfare departments were fully qualified. (Appendix M, p 336).

In addition to these there were another 100,000 workers, both manual and non-manual, employed in the services reviewed by Seebohm and very few of these had any social work training. Among those services with most qualified workers were the residential staff in children's homes and nurseries of whom *one in four* (out of 5,600) were trained. There were of course those with other forms of training including the 2,400 medical officers or school medical officers with medical training, and those working as home nurses, school nurses, domiciliary midwives or health visitors—over 20,000 in all—who had at least a basic nursing training, if not as in most cases a further qualification. The largest group, excluding residential staff, were some 30,000 home helps working under nearly nine hundred organizers. (Appendix L, p 329).

To obtain a comprehensive total of those in the social work field one should add some 1500 full time and 4000 part time youth leaders and the many trained and untrained, paid and unpaid, full time and part time workers in Citizens Advice Bureaux, Family Service Units, Marriage Guidance Councils, the WRVS, the churches, community associations and many other organisations. The community workers were under study by the Gulbenkian committee under Dame Eileen Younghusband and the voluntary workers by the committee headed by Miss Geraldine Aves. Nevertheless it was a pity that the Seebohm committee did not provide a comprehensive analysis of workers in the social services, both statutory and voluntary. It is unrealistic to plan for expansion without taking all the social work manpower into consideration. Shortage of workers is stressed throughout the Seebohm Report; for example, " It is clear that there is no hope in the foreseeable future of offering conventional psychiatric or social person to person service to all adults or children who are seriously maladjusted " (para 344) and " the entire social work staff now available to many local authorities could be usefully occupied solely in trying to support patients (suffering from severe mental disorder); helping them, their families and local committees to readjust " (para 346).

the curious desire for more and professional shortages

Despite our lack of clear knowledge about what social workers do and what they achieve, we still want more of them. " It is an interesting and often overlooked fact that, during the last twenty years, whenever the British people have identified and investigated a social problem, there has followed a national call for more social workers " (R. M. Titmuss, *Commitment to welfare*, p 85, Allen and Unwin, 1968 compare G. Steiner, *Social insecurity: the politics of welfare*, p 20, Rand McNally, Chicago, 1966, for a similar comment on events in the United States). No matter how intense the criticism of the services, the need for more trained social workers is unquestioned: more training and smaller caseloads remain the constant ideals. Both countries have experienced a constant shortage of social workers for many years.

Estimations and perceptions, or at least assumptions of shortage are common in the professions and can be determined by factors such as the changing pace of science with its new demands, the recognition of new needs, higher public expectations of the quality of services, the existence or creation of national structures with publicized personnel norms, a high rate of dropout of trainees, a high turnover of staff and perhaps the brevity of a professional career, particularly among women, the reduction of the work week, the employment of professional workers on " nonprofessional " duties such as administration. Many factors, therefore, in addition to the methods of utilization, affect perceptions of shortage for any occupational or professional group.

Acute shortages of trained workers have not been confined to the social work profession alone. In the nursing profession, for example, both Great Britain and the United States report an acute shortage of nurses; yet these two countries have two of the world's most favourable ratio of graduate nurses to population and the number of nurses has been increasing much faster than the populations in both countries. Indeed Glaser reports that " some graduate nursing officers of WHO — concerned with the practical service needs of countries and acclimatised to judging the actual problems of countries on the basis of objective statistics instead of national self-evaluations—do not think that Great Britain and America actually are short of nurses." (William A. Glaser in F. Davis (ed), *The nursing profession*, pp 32-33, Wiley, New York, 1966).

As Glaser points out, " occupations dedicated to the public service . . . usually seek more recruits and complain about shortages. These occupations are concerned with solving society's problems as defined by their own expert judgements, and the number of problems that exist (or that they think exist) invariably outruns the manpower. The incumbents have a vested interest in expansion: their social prestige rises as the popularity of their career grows, particularly among the ablest members of society." (*ibid* p 31). A very important factor determining demand may be the activity of the profession itself. "The national call for more social workers" referred to above seems very often to have been created, at least in part, by social workers and administrators. Indeed Titmuss' "British people" may well be the representatives of the profession, strengthened by those who do not want to transform the structure of society, but only the means of accommodating "problem groups" to the rest of society.

The public and private reaction of the vested interests to the Seebohm report cannot but heighten anxiety that a major function of the report has been to strengthen the position of the profession and of administrators. The committee itself consisted essentially of the various vested interests particularly from the National Institute of Social Work Training, the staff college of the social work profession. By the end it could be said to be represented by its chairman, its principal, one of its lecturers and perhaps too its president's wife—four out of ten.

geographical inequalities in services

One of the shortcomings of the social services and social work provision is the very uneven distribution of social workers across the country. This was well documented for some workers in the Seebohm report in Appendix G but it was given little attention in the body of the report. A strong argument for central government control is provided by this unevenness and Seebohm admits that the need for such control was argued "particularly clearly and forcefully" by an unspecified group of social workers, "the thought behind it was that the needs of the community would be better served by a comprehensive service, and that for administrative and financial reasons the present local authority structure would be inadequate to bear the weight of the service required" (para 137). The committee however gave this suggestion only one paragraph's discussion, mainly, apparently, because they understood their terms of reference as "implying that the services in question should remain the responsibility of local government." This at least is debatable but the committee apparently regarded the *des*cription "local authority . . . services" in the terms of reference also as a *pres*cription on its work.

Apart from the recommendations for special "priority areas for community development" or "social development areas" (paras 485-490), akin to Plowden's "educational priority areas" and the "areas of special housing need" advocated by the National Committee for Commonwealth Immigrants, the Seebohm Committee does not make any specific proposals for rectifying the unequal geographical distribution of social workers and social services. Yet a better national coverage is essential if an effective family service is really to be made " available for all."

This wider problem is discussed in part of one paragraph (490) and in the summary, at the end of the proposals for areas of special needs, the committee states " Central and local government, with the professions themselves, must accept responsibility for securing a better distribution of staff over the country as a whole " (p 230).

In 1962 local authorities' own estimates of their needs for social workers by 1972 varied widely, from 5 to 28 per 100,000 population in county boroughs and from 2 to 20 per 100,000 among the counties. Overall this represented an increase of 66 per cent over the ten years, from 2,940 to 4,880. In trying to estimate the need for trained staff, Paige and Jones decided that " needs are so various that a comprehensive estimate on the basis of numbers needing help would be impossible." (D. Paige and K. Jones, *Health and welfare services in Britain in* 1975, p 111, Cambridge University Press, 1966). As an alternative therefore they grouped local authorities with broadly similar social and economic characteristics together and estimated the provision that would be needed if the plans of all authorities were raised to the level of those 20 per cent in each group aiming at the most liberal facilities. This would mean an increase of not 66 per cent by 1972 but 145 per cent, giving a total of 7,200 social workers in the health and welfare services, almost half as many again as the local authorities' own estimates (*ibid*, p 112-113. Welfare assistants are omitted from the calculations in this paragraph and the next to enable comparison between reports).

The latest revised estimates of the local authorities still fall far short of that suggested by Paige and Jones. Although the estimates are markedly higher, because of encouraging recruitment figures, the forecast requirements for 1975 put forward in 1965 are still only 6,403. The need of 7,600 estimated by Paige and Jones for that year is still 20 per cent above that of the local authorities (*Health and welfare: the development of community care*, revision to 1975-76 of plans for the health and welfare services of the local authorities in England and Wales, p 14, cmnd 3022, HMSO, 1966).

the use of social workers

Quite clearly local authorities' own forecasts are mainly an extrapolation of their own present manpower. Very little attention has been given to the basic questions of the utilisation and deployment of trained and untrained staff, and the advantages that derive from the combination of different levels and types of staff. At least one body concerned with professional training, however, is worried about " an over-emphasis of the manpower needs of the service at the expense of the educational needs of the profession."

Dame Eileen Younghusband, for many years a leader of the social work profession, has insistently argued for greater attention to the actual use of social workers. She said very forcefully in 1951: " Sufficient attention has been given to the qualifications which employing bodies ' should ' require in comparison with *the quite insufficient attention given* to the much more pressing problem of how, in the present extreme shortage, trained and qualified workers can be used to the best advantage . . . and the job itself be so analysed and broken down that sledge-hammers are not wasted in cracking nuts, nor personal problems mishandled by the incompetent." (*Social work in Britain*, p 28, Carnegie UK Trust, my emphasis).

This demand was expressed clearly and vigorously again in the report of the committee she chaired from 1955 to 1959, and she stressed the urgency for this once more in 1965 (" A comparative view of manpower problems: the British approach," *Social service review*, pp 454-458, 1965).

But there is as yet, to my knowledge, no detailed analysis of the use of qualified as opposed to unqualified workers. The general impression is that the higher the training, the higher up the career structure the worker starts and the faster he climbs it. The less trained therefore are most likely to make the first and continuing contact with clients. This paradox deserves emphasis. Better training is advocated because it equips one best for the current dominant professional activity of case-work. Yet it seems that the general trend is for the better trained to have less contact with clients or customers, to have the greater administrative responsibilities, and so have less opportunity for practising the skills they have been taught. The extent to which this is compensated for by senior workers acting as supervisors or by providing in-service training is not clear and certainly deserves closer examination. At the best, at present, this is simply assumed to be so.

the use of time

With an inadequate provision and distribution of trained staff and a lack of facilities to increase the supply of trained staff fast enough, it is important to study the ways in which social workers deploy their own working hours. The 1959 Younghusband report found that one-third of the average working time of a heterogeneous body of field workers was spent on " letter-writing, record-keeping or other administrative procedures," one-fifth in travelling and about one-third to one-half in direct contact with the client. (para 397).

A more detailed study of the child care service in seven Scottish local authority departments in 1960 found that the social workers spent less time than they estimated on what they regarded as their major functions and more time than they thought on other activities. One quarter of the time was spent travelling, one-third on administration and one-third on paper work. In contrast preventive work only took up one-tenth of the time, children being received into care absorbing the greatest amount of work. Less than 2 hours a week was spent with children and only about one hour in conversation with them, including chats on journeys. " It seems that the professional worker's conception of his job involves a much greater application to the casework and therapeutic aspects of the service than his situation allows." (T. Burns and S. Sinclair, *The child care service at work,* p 42, Scottish Education Department, Edinburgh, 1963).

A study of newly-qualified medical social workers found that they spent between a third and a half of their time on work which did not require professional training either in their view or that of their heads of department (E. M. Moon and K. M. Slack, *The first two years,* Institute of Medical Social Workers, 1965).

Similar findings emerged from a medical social work department study at the Hammersmith Hospital (Z. Butrym, *Medical social work in action,* Bell 1968). It was agreed that an administrative or welfare assistant could in fact handle this work just as efficiently with considerable saving of resources, especially the time of trained staff.

Analysis of the working time of other professionals outside social work might well lead to similar conclusions but this does not weaken the significance of such findings. First, the demands placed on workers distracting them, so to speak, from the job they are employed, trained and publicly and professionally expected to do, can lead to acute dissatisfaction, increase the turnover rate, result in long and irregular hours and generally lower standards of efficiency. Yet the extent of these non-professional demands are often not recognised by those outside the work-group, leading to conflict between the workers and administrators. (see John Haines, " Satisfaction in social work," *New Society,* 5 January 1967).

In the end the major sufferers are the clients and those would-be clients who are not seen because of the lack of time. The workers have insufficient time to explain to clients what is happening or just to listen to them. Often secretarial staff, not only unqualified but inexperienced, are left to hold the fort and bear the brunt of many initial tension-ridden contacts with a department. In addition, when workers do fall ill or leave, it is often the poorest areas of a town that go longest without a replacement, workers being transferred to fill gaps elsewhere. In one local authority I was told by other social workers that the most " inadequate " social workers were most likely to be dumped in the slum areas. As one man put it " If you let

him loose in a respectable area, the office would be inundated with complaints."
Once again the poor are the losers.

The very important role played by office staff, even when completely untrained,
has been revealed in a number of sociological studies of organisations. Receptionists
in an American state employment exchange exercised considerable discretion in
handling applicants for work, although they were only clerical employees and formal
criteria which circumscribed their powers had been very carefully laid down. Their
function was to limit the flow of applicants for jobs, and their code of procedures
laid down the date on which they should tell applicants to return (P. M. Blau,
The dynamics of bureaucracy, pp 28-34 and 87-90, Chicago University press,
revised edition, 1963). In another American study the application clerk in an urban
housing department exercised considerable control over whether or not those
coming in to her desk were eventually found the equivalent of a council house;
in fact some would-be applicants never got further than her desk. " Whether or
not the prospective applicant becomes an eligible applicant, whether or not the
eligible applicant can hope to become a tenant, and in which project he is most
likely to become a tenant—all of these depend, in large part, upon the impression
he makes on the gatekeeper at the initial contact." (I. Deutscher " The gatekeeper
in public housing," *Among the people: encounters with the urban poor*, p 40, Basic
Books, New York, 1968).

RECOMMENDATIONS FOR POLICY

So far I have tried to point out the deficiencies in our knowledge about the practice
of social work, the strengths and weaknesses that we do know, the conflict and
uncertainty over what social workers should be doing and the anxiety that many,
for one reason or another, are at present becoming more agents of social control
than of social welfare. Clearly we need better information and a wider and more
vigorous debate about the role of social workers and the social services in Britain.
But while the debating and data-collecting continue, decisions have to be taken
now on the existing evidence, meagre as it is, and on the basis of current ideas
and accumulated experience. These decisions may well shape the nature and distribution of the practice of social work for many years to come.

re-deployment and substitutability

The government must take hard, and probably professionally unpopular, decisions
about the redeployment and substitutability of workers in different services and
at different levels. Dame Eileen Younghusband has been demanding this since 1951.

With scarce resources how do we deploy our social workers? The evidence suggests that we should employ more home helps, welfare assistants and auxiliaries and extend this part of the service much faster than the numbers of fully qualified social workers. At once we are led into difficult and sensitive areas where one has to weigh the values of one service against another. This of course is a familiar problem for the professions: a major question in the field of medicine is the allocation of resources and personnel to what can be crudely differentiated as curative and preventive medicine. In fact in both the medical and social work professions those more involved in curative work have tended to have higher pay and status and greater power and influence. Only when they agree has it usually been possible to increase less skilled staff (compare also the teaching profession's reaction to teaching aides).

problems of professional demarcation

Every doctor, social worker, teacher and nurse in this country is well aware of the disruptive effect on the economy of semi-skilled manual workers arguing for weeks as to who drills the hole. Isn't it ridiculous? I mean I can drill a hole; can't you? Does it matter who drills it? Why can't the trade unions learn to live in peace —like *us*? The truth is that the country has been constantly held to ransom by the professions and the so-called professions—and the costs of the ransom have been paid most heavily by those least equipped to pay.

Amongst the professions public disputes are usually avoided. There is a gentleman's agreement that "dog does not bite dog" supported by nicely-phrased terms of reference and by professional decorum. Each report, public or private, on a profession therefore does not rock the boat — the Royal Commission on Medical Education, the (Salmon) Report of the Committee on Senior Nursing Staff Structure and now Seebohm and even Gulbenkian. Each report in its own blinkered way bears out the wisdom and insight of Everett Hughes when he writes about the professions, and the way in which the rest of society pays increasing heed to them. Each establishes a little wider the professional empire.

The Royal Commission on Medical Education, for example, does not include nurses in its index and even the few references in the text pay relatively slight attention to the ways in which their deployment affects the demand for medical staff. The four indexed references to social workers show equal neglect of the potential contribution that can be made by these workers either inside or outside hospitals that would have implications for the use of scarce medical staff, and indeed two of the references seem concerned simply to differentiate the roles of doctors and social workers.

The possibilities therefore for redeployment are handicapped, first by our lack of knowledge about what workers with different levels and types of skills do and achieve, and second by the resistance to transferring responsibilities out of one's own jurisdiction, if it involves professional rivalries. Yet the actual responsibilities of professionally qualified social workers include much that might be allocated to others. There appear to be strong grounds for a reorganisation of the types of work carried out and for more emphasis, and increased recognition and status, to be given to the roles of welfare assistant, information officer, administrative assistant, home help and home help organiser and so on.

A recent survey of thirteen local authority areas of the services for the elderly concluded that in most areas " the home help service and housing programmes could be at least doubled without resulting in overprovision." (A. I. Harris, *Social welfare for the elderly*, Government Social Survey, vol 1, p 65, HMSO 1968). This conclusion did not allow for any increase in the time home helps provided the elderly, nor for the vast expansion of home help numbers if my suggestion is accepted. A lot could be done to enable social workers to meet the community's needs by job-analysis. Faced with a demand for a 25 per cent increase in its nursing staff, some eight or nine times the generally allowed national increase, one local authority analysed the work of the nursing staff. By stepping up the number of home-helps, they were able to meet the demand which had in fact genuinely increased: the excess demand for nursing staff was due to nurses lighting fires, doing shopping and much of the work that is usually done by home helps. The displacement of low-skill tasks to lower-paid workers may usually be made acceptable to the higher-trained, provided that other differentials are maintained and the work displaced is of lower status. Dirty work is conventionally low status (although, as occupational sociologists point out, dirty work is all right provided it is accompanied by high status and high pay, the surgeon providing a particularly good example).

early and easy contact

The detailed study of substitutability and interchange in the social service occupations and professions should be combined with the problem of how the customer is enabled to reach services that have a tendency to withdraw into the confines of bureaucratic organisation. Here the roles of the general practitioner, the health visitor, the supplementary benefits officer and the police in the community, the nurse in the hospital and the teacher in the school are of vital importance. These are the people already best placed to inform people of their rights and to recognise unmet needs. The health visitor is a particularly good example of a relatively low status—though highly-trained—worker who can play a tremendous role in alerting consumers of the services available. Unfortunately the current trend seems to move away from these people in either direction—towards " grass roots " organisations on the one hand, and towards large co-ordinated social units on the other. Here too "lower-grade" workers like home helps or voluntary visitors can achieve a great deal. Over one-quarter of a million people live in institutions and they become all too easily isolated from the rest of the community. Untrained workers can help many of these residents, especially ensuring that they do not become isolated from the benefits and services available to the rest of the community. An extension of workers such as home-helps and welfare assistants could enable many people to stay in their own homes in their own community (see E. Shanas et al, *op cit*, Peter Townsend, *The last refuge*, and Jeremy Tunstall, *Old and alone*, Routledge and Kegan Paul, 1966).

the nurse-social worker in the hospital and the community

A more radical suggestion may be made for the employment of nurse-social workers who could not only improve the quality of services available to the patient and his family while he is in hospital but could do much to break down the gap between hospital and community that makes a mockery of many of the pretentions of community care programmes. Often hospital nurses unequipped with social work knowledge have to deal with social work problems. The comfort of the ill and the dying, the giving of information to the patient and his family, particularly the diagnosis of an illness with little hope of recovery or which will mean great adjustments both for the patient and his family—these are all tasks that many nurses have to undertake. Yet they receive very little, if any, training that equips them for this work, which is very demanding and imposes a considerable strain on many. Once again this raises the important question of what happens to the people who need social work help but do not receive it, or at least not from the appointed worker, whether trained or not. Careful analysis of the work actually done by medical social workers might enable much of value to be incorporated in the training of nurses. Ward sisters complain about the appointment of part-time medical social workers who handle "their" problems on Mondays but have to leave the sister or a junior nurse to manage these same problems for the rest of the week. (Some social workers sometimes talk of the ignorance of nurses without any awareness of the extent to which their own type of work is being carried out by this generally lower-paid and lower-status occupation). Much could be achieved by providing nurses with some of the knowledge necessary to handle these problems with greater ease and effectiveness.

Already a three-month period in community or home nursing is included in the basic training of some twelve groups of pupil nurses and five of student nurses. This does not of course equip a nurse for social work but the knowledge of patients as people with families living in their homes, and the better appreciation of their problems this provides, makes them more aware of both the need for, and scope of, medical social work. There will probably be two benefits for the patient. First, the nurse will be more sensitive to the needs of patients and their families and better able to understand their anxieties and problems. Secondly, the nurse should be better able to realise that a patient has particular problems and would be more willing to refer patients to medical social workers.

In providing support for the psychiatric patient with his family at home and at work there is already strong support from the Mental Nurses Committee of the General Nursing Council for the nurse to take a more active part. Any demarcation dispute with the psychiatric social worker and the mental welfare officer seems unlikely because there are, and will continue to be, insufficient numbers of either worker. There is the additional advantage that the nurse may have known a patient as a member of the psychiatric ward family for six months, a year or longer and can offer help to avert the need for readmission because of the relationship created. Out-patient nursing has in fact been provided in Croydon by Warlingham Park Hospital since 1954. Qualified mental nurses have been seconded to provide after-care for patients in the community who can therefore be discharged earlier, to look after patients who may have relapsed and new patients not believed to need in-patient care (A. R. May and S. Moore, " The mental nurse in the community," *The Lancet*, 26 January 1963). These nurses have not only worked in closer contact with the community services including social workers but they have themselves undertaken what might be described as basic social work in providing support for the patients, relieving the anxieties of relative by timely explanations and putting them in touch with the social services when necessary.

In hospitals and homes for the mentally subnormal there is an even stronger case for nurses playing the role of nurse-social worker. Relatively little physical nursing has to be done but much help needs to be provided for the family of the patient, and in many cases a trained worker can do much to help the patient's progress. The significance of the part that could be played by nurses with some quite basic training is revealed by a recent study of thirty-four institutions for the mentally subnormal. Over half the patients were in institutions without social workers and none of the twenty-two employed had a full professional qualification and nine had neither training of any type nor any previous experience. This indicates, incidentally, the low status given such jobs by trained social workers. (Pauline Morris, *Put away*, Routledge and Kegan Paul, 1970).

Surprisingly a textbook on social work with the mentally subnormal pays no attention to the nurses beyond an occasional reference to " skilled nursing " although there are a number of references to doctors. The author does not point out the very small amount of medical care received by the mentally subnormal. (F. Joan Todd, *Social work with the mentally subnormal*. Routledge and Kegan Paul). It seems likely that the greater involvement of the nurses with the patients and their

D

families would do much to develop the understanding of the nurses and improve their own view of their role and the importance of their work. It would also help to promote links with the community outside the institution and help to break down the barrier that seems to be so much greater for many of these institutions. This sharing of social work knowledge could also be of value for the teaching profession.

the medical social worker in the community

The introduction of the nurse-social worker would enable a greater provision of medical social workers for general practice, particularly Health Centres. Since " perhaps 90 per cent of all illness " that comes to the notice of the medical profession is dealt with " entirely within the ambit of general practice " (Royal Commission on medical education, para 325, HMSO 1968), both preventive and curative work of great value could presumably be provided by social workers at this point. The interim report of the Caversham project in Camden suggests the great value of the role that may be played by a social worker based in a group practice.

While increasing success seems to be achieved by medical social work units outside hospitals, many social workers in the hospitals still encounter considerable difficulties in reaching the patients when they are needed, essentially because of a lack of an efficient referral system as well as a shortage of workers full time in many hospitals, or their employment on work not really needing a fully trained social worker. It seems unlikely that medical social workers in hospitals can overcome the barriers facing them very quickly, even where they are relatively highly concentrated. And there is still the problem that many hospitals or hospital units have only a part time social worker and some have none at all, as the mental subnormality institutions described above. In 1966 about one-third of qualified and practising medical social workers were concentrated in about one-tenth of the hospitals employing any medical social workers at all. (My analysis of Institute of Medical Social Workers' List of Members, January 1967). It appears then that every encouragement should be given by the government for local authorities to employ medical social workers on a much greater scale and appoint them, where possible and appropriate, to general practices. Although others may be opposed, the results of research so far suggests that this may do much to promote the quality of care for the patient and will improve access and provide early contact for those in need of social workers' help.

social work training

Many of Seebohm's recommendations about training should be implemented as soon as possible, and their basic emphasis is repeated in the Gulbenkian committee's report on *Community work and social change*. It is important that social workers should in their training learn more about group and community work and more about the dynamics of society and social change. But too much stress must not again be placed on teaching new techniques, skills and methods of manipulation of the client—whether it be individual, family, group or community.

Social workers need to know more about the intricacies of the rent acts and of rent rebate schemes and much more about the lives of those they have to serve. In their training at present their contact ouside the worker-client setting with what one might describe as the population at risk of being clients is very limited. Essentially they need to be able to develop during training a view of their role as servants of the community with responsibilities that are more socially-oriented.

the teaching of " human relations "

At the same time the experience of social workers should be spread as widely as possible throughout the community. Knowing more about the way people react to crises, illness, disability or handicap, to material or emotional problems will help all servants of the public in front-line organisations to cope with their own impulses and reactions and will lessen the strain and tension under which the majority of them have to work. This knowledge should not be jealously guarded and kept locked up with the professionally qualified worker in a room all too often guarded by a completely untrained receptionist.

This is not to say that we should all become social workers, but it is to argue that social workers' knowledge is not just commonsense. An understanding of human behaviour in health, illness and crisis is valuable for these staff workers. The Royal Commission on Medical Education argued for doctors, " all students should be taught to recognise the effects of their own behaviour upon others " and they should have some knowledge of " the social and cultural factors which influence patients' response." (paras 254 and 257). This seems equally true for all workers in the social services.

Eugene Heimler has done much to pioneer courses providing such training. The help that Heimler was able to give National Assistance recipients in Hendon who had been out of work for at least two years *and* were thought by officers to have serious emotional problems shows what can be achieved by a social caseworker (E. Heimler, *Mental illness and social work,* chap 7, Penguin, 1967). But the particular significance of the Hendon experiment is that it took social work knowledge out into the community. With Heimler's help the National Assistance Board began in 1958 to provide a part time training course for their executive officers related to the practical day-to-day work of officers. " One of its important aims was not only to impart knowledge about human relations and family behaviour, but also to allow the members to see their own prejudices and reactions to their clients in a new light." (*ibid*, p 144). These courses have had great success. The reactions of the officers "as expressed on paper read, in fact, so much like testimonials for a patent medicine that the scepticism which fills the heart of all administrators was overflowing." (K. R. Stowe, "Staff training in the National Assistance Board: problems and policies," *Public Administration*, Winter 1961). By 1964 some seventeen universities were providing "Human Relations" courses and similar part time training programmes have been introduced for employment exchange officials and certain local authority staff.

training for the doorkeepers

The Seebohm report does not make any reference to this work. It does, however, briefly acknowledge the need for some training at all levels in the social service departments. "It would be a great mistake to concentrate on the training of field social workers and senior administrative officers and to forget . . . that the whole organisation will depend among other things on an efficient and sympathetic telephone service" (para 529). The rest of the chapter on training however, makes scant reference to such problems. The training of the receptionists or telephonists gains added importance if departments are to be co-ordinated. As shown earlier, these workers can do much to determine not only the initial attitude of an incomer to a department but also the way in which the client is eventually treated. It is vital that these workers should have a good knowledge of the services available at their office which can save the customer considerable time, for example waiting in vain for an interview higher up or having to repeat one's story unnecessarily. This is of immense significance to a woman with three boisterous and fidgety young children with her or who has left them with a neighbour and is anxious about exhausting her good-will. Such workers should also have some basic knowledge of human relations that will enable them to put visitors at their ease and to cope with particularly anxious, excitable or even aggressive visitors.

These courses could well be extended to many others working in organisations involving contact with the public such as the police, employment exchange officers and of course the nurses whose possible new role I described above.

the emphasis on "social" work

In the courses for all levels of workers, additional emphasis must be placed on the social aspect of the social workers' job which has been so much neglected. The responsibility of the servant to his customer and the community needs to be clearly established and the conflicts that will often ensue be admitted and discussed. Social workers of course are not the only public servants who have tended to forget their responsibility to the individual, the family and the community in their concern to avoid offending their employer or the apparently much dreaded " tax-payer," but they are among the highest-trained and best-paid to do so. It is all the more sad in their case because of the stress in their ideology on meeting the individual needs of their clients.

THE ROLE OF A SOCIAL WORKER

Earlier I put forward a tentative definition of the role of the social worker. If his work is going to meet these requirements, then it is important that he should be able to act as a social investigator, and as a mediator and interpreter.

the social worker as social investigator

In 1920 Clement Attlee described " social investigation " as " a particular form of social work " (*The social worker,* Bell, London). " It is not possible," he said, " for the ordinary rank and file of social workers to hope to rival skilled investigators, but each one can take his part by cultivating habits of careful observation and analysis of the pieces of social machinery that come under his notice." (p 230). No-one can foresee all the effects, direct and indirect, of any change in policy and therefore it is vital to compare achievement with intention and watch for any side-effects. This sort of role is currently being performed, magnificently and, one is often told, quite " unprofessionally " by such indiscreet amateurs in Citizens' Advice Bureaux as Audrey Harvey who, except in Attlee's sense, is not perhaps a social worker. It is interesting, and important, to note that Attlee cites the operation of minimum wage legislation as an example of where social workers might keep a watchful eye.

In fact social workers were instrumental in helping Tawney's study of minimum work-rates; but how many social workers today are aware that nearly one in five of the establishments inspected by the nation's 140 wage inspectors are paying below the statutory wage to at least some of their employees? (See the summary of statistics published annually in the *Employment and Productivity Gazette*). Also social workers need to be reminded that it was while he was working as a social worker at Toynbee Hall that Beveridge produced his seminal and influential work on unemployment which remains unrivalled today. This work investigated causes and suggested preventives and did not deal only with symptoms and palliatives, immediate and temporary.

This role of social investigation and reporting back of the faults should be a vital part of social work today. To quote Attlee once again, " The demand of the social reformer today is for a new attitude to social problems rather than for specific reforms in any particular department of life." (p 13). This, of course, immediately brings into question again the " objective " or " politically neutral " role of the social worker and the injection of his own values into his work.

The major way in which this role can be extended is by providing organisations like the Citizens' Advice Bureaux with more resources and better trained staff. They have however to make themselves better known to the public and more accessible, with longer opening hours and often better-placed and more attractive offices. There seem to be strong grounds for experimenting with the community shops that appear to have been one of the more successful parts of the American action programmes. The argument for an independent " consumer shop " is made strongly by Lucy Syson and Rosalind Brooke (" The voice of the consumer," *More power to the people,* eds. B. Lapping and G. Radice, Longmans, 1968).

The supportive and feedback role of the social worker can be developed in many other ways. Home-helps are particularly well-placed to inform those they visit of the other services available. They should also be encouraged to report when they come across those who have needs that cannot be met by the services known to them. Only in ways such as these can the services adjust of their own accord to meet unmet needs; rather than give away unwillingly, after outside pressure. Small-scale research on certain groups is also valuable in disclosing where needs are not met. A recent small, and relatively inexpensive, study revealed the extent of poverty and the extent of ignorance about rights and services amongst residents in a small area of Liverpool. At the same time it provided valuable education to the participants. Interviewing 208 families, analysis of the data and publication involved some seventy members of the group and provided a quick but valuable knowledge of the intricacies of social service provision. " By the third night of the project, group members who had been slightly bemused by the mass of benefits available, were conversing knowledgeably on topics ranging from rate rebates to free spectacles." (Peter Moss, *Welfare rights project* 1968, p 3, Merseyside Child Poverty Action Group, February 1969).

the social worker as mediator and interpreter

As the organisation of the social services and society in general becomes more complex and intricate, many people need help in finding out their rights or just the alternatives open to them in many complicated situations. Where the social worker is easily identifiable and approachable, he can play a very important role in interpreting bureaucratic regulations or mediating between a family and some organisation. In some towns at least people will approach the NSPCC officer—" the cruelty man "—for advice on many different issues completely unrelated to his job —to solve matrimonial disputes, to explain the details of a hire-purchase agreement or to persuade a firm to set payments at a lower level, to intervene with a local social worker or to settle arguments with the income tax-authorities. (Rodgers and Dixon, *Portrait of Social Work*, p 151, Oxford University Press, 1960, and observed by me on Tyneside and in parts of London). And of course such difficulties are often raised with the social worker who is visiting a family.

Once again this involves putting emphasis on the social worker's knowledge of the various systems and stresses his willingness to try to find out about such issues when asked rather than to refer the questioner onwards. This too is to emphasise the responsibility of the worker to the community rather than to his employing organisation: it involves a view of social work as a detached counter-profession. This is in part to put forward an argument for more group and community workers, but it is *not only* these workers that can act as a mediator between the individual and the local community and the local or central bureaucracy. Indeed one hopes that one of the strengths of greater professionalism among all types of social workers will be their greater willingness to stand up on behalf of those they are expected to serve.

the danger of disfranchisement

Despite this basically optimistic view of the role that the social worker can play, it must be admitted that the greater opportunities for promoting welfare mean greater power. Indeed the ever-growing numbers of social workers and government officials that are in contact with the families, mainly of the working-class, exercise a great amount, an increasing amount, of power. As yet the citizen has very little defence against them. Our ombudsman—the Parliamentary Commissioner—cannot intervene in local government decisions nor in the many discretionary decisions of public officials. There is the danger that certain sections of the community may be disfranchised in the sense that their " social control " is entrusted to the appropriate agency, its administrators and its field workers.

If one unified social service department is introduced, then the problem of offering families some protection seems even more urgent. It is unrealistic to argue that families do not need such defence: social workers are as fallible as the rest of us and there is always bound to be a variation in quality. One must accept that some families' road to hell has been paved with the good intentions of social workers. To an extent some right of appeal already exists in bodies such as the Mental Health Review Tribunals but they are really best suited for either-or situations: should this man be committed to, or remain in a mental hospital or not? They are likely to be of less use in controlling the everyday discretionary actions of social workers. One of the critical facts to realise is that a client expects to remain in touch with a particular social worker. He is well aware that it will be the same caseworker who will continue to take decisions that may affect him vitally. As Joel Handler has argued, the client " is beginning to think that in the ' long run ' it would be 'better' for her family if she agreed with the caseworker." (Joel F. Handler, "Controlling official behaviour in welfare administration," in Jacobus Ten Broek (ed), *The law of the poor*, Chandler, San Francisco, 1966). In fact it is the power of the worker that may largely nullify in this respect any programme of rights. "Before rights can be made effective . . . there has to be knowledge, ability or resources, *and clear, practical advantages for using these rights." (ibid*, p 171, emphasis in the original).

This situation is of course one common to the service professions and no clear solution to it has yet been developed. This however does seem to be a major area in which professional development, which would raise the standards expected of a worker and would perhaps lay down an ethical code, might benefit the client. This will not be solved easily: how in fact can one define " malpractice " in social work? But much could be done to indicate the responsibilities of workers in taking discretionary action. (See Kathleen Bell, *Tribunals in the social services*, Routledge and Kegan Paul, 1969).

Clearly some more formal protection will have to be provided: at the moment much of the burden of this work is accepted by local councillors or local MPs, but success depends very much on the time, energy, resources and personal charm or " pull " of the individual. Another ombudsman for such matters, or a committee to replace the existing Parliamentary Commissioner which would have powers to investigate, if necessary, any action of a public employee seems essential. The opportunity for making complaints should also be made much easier and not be dependent upon first convincing one's MP that there are grounds for complaint.

a more equal geographical distribution

None of these developments, changes in emphasis, reforms or attempts to promote access or maintain quality will be of much significance if we cannot ensure a much more equal distribution of resources—social workers and services—across the whole country. The type and extent of help families and individuals living in different parts of the country receive should not be affected by the accidents of residence and historical development or by the poverty in resources, imagination, administrative skill, political infighting or simple humanity of their local authority. To take a particularly graphic example, Rotherham spends £483 per thousand of its population on home helps while Tynemouth, of roughly similar size, spends less than £17 (Jean Packman, *Child care: needs and numbers*, Allen and Unwin). The responsibility for a geographically even provision rests with the central government for it is part of the very essence of a democracy that the services it can provide should exist in reality for all citizens. The social work professional associations can do much to help by encouraging their members to recognise this need for an even service and by working with local and central government to devise effective schemes that will help to spread our scarce supply of social workers across the country, as in fact the medical profession has very greatly succeeded in improving the distribution of doctors in general practice.

agitation and responsibility

" Every social worker is almost certain to be also an agitator. If he or she learns social facts and believes that they are due to certain causes which are beyond the power of an individual to remove, it is impossible to rest contented with the limited amount of good that can be done by following old methods and agitation to get people to see a new point of view." These words were written in 1920 in a book entitled *The Social Worker* by Clement Attlee, then a lecturer in social administration at the London School of Economics. This emphasis on the responsibilities of the social worker for social reform were of course written before psychoanalysis did so much to neutralise the profession's social conscience.

An increasing stress on the need for social reform and social action is appearing in much social work today, although often in the face of vigorous opposition. As Attlee went on to say, " The word ' agitator ' is distrustful to many; it calls up a picture of a person who is rather unbalanced, honest perhaps, but wrongheaded, possibly dishonest, troubling the waters with a view to fishing in them for his own benefit. This is mainly the point of view of the person who is on the whole contented with things as they are . . ."

A persistent and searching attitude will involve the social worker constantly in the whole debate about what sort of society we want. What do we mean by democracy and participation? What are rights and needs—how are they published and provided or recognised and met? How do we open up, rather than close, channels of communication not just between agencies under the cure-all term of " co-ordination " but between citizens, consumers and providers, between and among the professions, between the rich and the poor? Social workers cannot opt out of this continuing debate. By ignoring such questions, they will only help to preserve existing divisions within society and may well promote new ones. These are the issues which in the end must dominate the discussion over policy. Basically, I am arguing that social workers in our social services today must accept a greater responsibility for the significance of their actions in a society characterised by persistent or even increasing inequality for many groups. No social worker can be neutral in his or her daily actions: if he believes he can be, then he is simply acquiescing, as Attlee said, in " things as they are."

A government, especially a Labour one, should be prepared to accept a responsibility to support and encourage social work of the types I have suggested. The government and the social work professions must recognise that the skills of social workers should be attuned to the needs of the citizens, and not, as seems to have happened so often, the citizens' needs be redefined to fit the social workers' own special concerns, or departments' own convenient administrative pigeonholes. The immediate and persistent objectives of policy must be to make the knowledge and skills of a more socially-oriented social work profession more available to the community, both by increasing the accessibility of social workers and by sharing some of their work and knowledge with others in the community. Redeployment of scarce resources, support and substitution with other workers and a better distribution of these services throughout society are essential if social work is to play a significant role in modern, industrialised society.

The social worker's responsibility is heavy. He has to act as interpreter and mediator for the citizen, as the reporter of social needs, the worker on the spot who is able to alert administrators and policy makers to the appearance of new problems and the resurgence of old ones. If he is not prepared to accept this role, then the poor, the weak, the helpless and their families and children must bear the costs, once more, silently and invisibly.

3. the child care service

Barbara Kahan

From the inside the child care service has always felt as though it were in the melting pot. To have tried to predict its future before a government statement of intent on the Seebohm Report and the re-organisation of the health services would justifiably have been considered rash, for not only child care but the whole future social service pattern largely depends on a definition of boundaries between these two areas of activity. They in their turn, are bound up with the future of local government and the relationships between it and central government. Nevertheless there have been clear indications of the role the child care service might play in the future even though the setting in which it would be played was uncertain. These indications were implicit in the past and present pattern of the service as well as in additional future responsibilities mapped out for it by the Children and Young Persons Act, 1969.

roots and growing points

When the child care service began in 1948 it must have seemed to many likely to remain an insignificant part of reconstructed postwar social services. The opposition to it argued that measures to deal with a comparatively small and special need such as the care of deprived children should be part of wider and existing provisions. Yet the setting up of a separate child care service can now be seen as an important step in a process leading logically to the Seebohm Report and the Bill which is likely to become the Local Authority Social Services Act, 1970. Through this social work will at last establish its independence as a parallel, not subsidiary, professional service with health and education and in so doing, will owe a good deal to the sense of conviction and determination of the child care service in pursuing this aim.

Children now have greater importance in English national life than formerly. Their early years are accepted as a period of growth, development and education during which satisfactory experiences in family life, school and leisure are likely to lay foundations for adequate adult functioning. This period during which potential is developing, may be productive of good or ill results and the implications of this fact have been increasingly used as arguments for investment in the young, and through them, in the future. Although our actions sometimes belie it, we tend, as a nation, to believe that services to children will produce a major investment return and that the converse may lead to such deficit factors as mental illness, delinquency and social inadequacy in adult life. The *raison d'etre* of the child care service in 1948 was to break with the past and to develop new and better provisions and methods of care for children whose family life had been disrupted or was inadequate and unsuitable for their upbringing. Thus not only a humane expression of society's concern would be offered but some of the worse results of deprivation might be avoided. The service was supported and strengthened by a centrally subsidised professional training programme which was unique in publicly administered social work.

Soon after 1948, joint circulars issued by the Home Office, Ministry of Education and Ministry of Health drew attention to the connection between neglect of children in their own homes and development of delinquency, maladjustment and poor general functioning, and local authorities were urged to co-ordinate voluntary and statutory social services in the interests of neglected children in their own homes. Co-ordination of social services has now become a general aim, but it started as a rallying cry about children and was still concerned with them at the time of the Ingleby Report in 1960 and the Children and Young Persons Act, 1963, which implemented it.

Much earlier, the Curtis Committee in 1945-6 had urged that the child care service should have very wide responsibilities. A Children's Officer was to be " a specialist in child care as the Medical Officer of Health is a specialist in his own province and the Director of Education in his." (*Report of the Care of Children Committee*, 1946, cmnd 6922, para 443). The Women's Group on Public Welfare studying children neglected in their own homes in 1946-7 recommended a " comprehensive service of care for all children " to be exercised through the new Children's Committees. (*The neglected child and his family*, p 125, recommendation 9, OUP 1948). This comprehensive service would have brought together much that Seebohm recommended for inclusion in a unified local authority social service and which will now be brought together by the 1970 Act. In fact, the logic of starting further back than family breakdown was so obvious that " preventive work " with families in the community first began in children's departments as early as 1949. (*First annual report, Children's officer Dudley*, 1950).

a complex task

Meanwhile, it soon became apparent that child care social workers, field or residential, had a very complex task. Each year since 1948 thousands of children have received short term care for reasons of their mothers' physical incapacity through illness or confinements (23,965 in twelve months ending 31 March, 1969) but, at the same time, many others (64,573 in 1968-69) are receiving long term care for a variety of reasons ranging from death or desertion of parents to homelessness, cruelty, removal from home on court orders as offenders or beyond control, illegitimacy, rejection and general neglect or lack of social and emotional support. Unlike the pre-1948 approach to them the families of children in care are also regarded as very important. They may complicate residential work and boarding out but their involvement is essential to the children's welfare. The child care service has authority problems similar to those faced by probation officers and in dealing with the family consequences of physical and mental illness, it faces the same problems as medical and psychiatric social workers. In addition it has a variety of other tasks involving courts, committees, public meetings of many kinds, providing an adoption service, working with voluntary societies and approved schools, caring for nineteen and twenty year olds in and out of hostels, and finding varied means of help and accommodation for children through the total intelligence range and with every kind of handicap in addition to the personal and social deprivation which had led to their initial referral. Two other factors have complicated the role of the child care service; first, the local authority setting in which it operates. This involves much more lay participation than other social work services experience, and willingness of lay members to delegate decision making or accept professional advice and interpretation of human problems has been variable. The second factor has been the built-in statutory obligation to provide a service even though resources and manpower were often not commensurate with demand. Important though the statutory obligation is, it has sometimes led to conflict between attempts to provide good standards and to meet demand which was too great for available resources.

illuminating need

For all these reasons the child care service rapidly became aware of deficiencies in other services as well as its own. It also learned something of the " political " background of distribution of resources, local authority balances of power, the need for a service to be comprehensible to lay representatives whose interest in it might be less than absorbing, and last but not least, the effect on individual children and their families of administrative and political decisions made in settings only remotely connected with their problems. These were experiences which were not available to the majority of other professional social workers. It is not accidental that amongst the professional groups now involved in forming the British Association of Social Workers and represented in the Seebohm Implementation Action Group child care workers are amongst the most politically aware and active.

The growth of the child care service since 1948 has been considerable. Statistics of staffing are not readily available and are not comprehensive, but the increase in field staff from a few hundreds in 1948 to three and a half thousand twenty years later is indicative. Other pointers are a massive development in training, a large body of additional legislation over the years, and the very high, and rising, numbers of children and young persons referred for help, advice and guidance each year. In the period 1 April, 1968—31 March, 1969, this figure was 308,076 in an estimated population of 13,350,000 under 18 years of age, a rate of twenty three in every thousand in a twelve months period. These figures do not include nearly 18,000 privately placed foster children and children involved in adoption, 7,500 in approved schools and more than as many out on licence or under supervision, nor several thousands more being supervised in the community under various legal requirements.

The Children and Young Persons Act, 1963, in particular has led to great expansion of the service. It was heralded by Members of Parliament of both Houses and both main parties as a measure which might not only prevent neglect and un-happiness for many children, but might go far, if adequately implemented, to prevent juvenile offending too. Initial attitudes to the new powers were ambivalent, both inside and outside the children's service, particularly those powers which enabled cash to be spent to avoid the need for children's reception into care. If rent arrears could be paid by the Children's Committees to keep children at home, would anyone ever pay rent again? Was it ethically sound to allow debtors to go " un-punished " by paying their debts for them and how far would fecklessness receive a new incentive to continue or increase? The amount of cash spent by Children's Committees under this Act has been relatively little in fact, but general experience of using the new powers has vividly illuminated many other social problems, such as housing shortages, policies in allocating housing, social security limits and distribution and social attitudes to such minority groups as unmarried mothers. Many examples of rigid compartmentalism in the social services have also been found and contributed to evidence given to the Seebohm Committee. Concentration of effort and thought on a wide variety of situations in which children and young persons were emotionally or socially deprived or at risk has, in fact, tended to high-light the needs of a larger section of the child population. The numbers of those who have actually come into contact with the children's service in some way may well, over 21 years, be between two and three millions. Although this figure is much smaller than the numbers with whom schools or local health services are in contact, the children's background situations have been more intimately known and recorded in more detail. In some areas too, the clientele of the child care service is drawn from all classes and income groups. These cases demonstrate that social class and wealth are no guarantee against emotional deprivation and neglect, even though material needs may be met. Sometimes rather the contrary appears to be true.

children in trouble

Parliament has now placed further responsibilities on the child care service under the Children and Young Persons Act, 1969, an Act which gives effect to the main proposals of the White Paper *Children in trouble*. The intention of this was to remove from the courts as many children and young persons as possible and to deal with and help them through their families and the social services, acting on the belief that few children in the course of growing up do not offend against the law but that when they do offend, what is needed is care, not punishment.

What effect will this legislation have on the child care service? The most obvious effect will be to bring many more children and young persons within its direct influence and responsibility. The number dealt with each year may be more than doubled and many of them will be those on whom society tends to frown. Police and child care workers will have to work much more closely together and child care will eventually take on all work formerly carried out by the probation service with boys and girls under 14. It will also play a much larger part than formerly in supervision of those over 14 and under 17. In addition, since approved school orders will be abolished all boys and girls under 17 removed from home will be committed to the care of children's departments.

Approved schools in many cases will become part of the range of residential facilities organised and provided by the local authorities' child care service. At present few residential establishments for children and young people outside the approved school system provide " secure accommodation." Liberalising legislation affecting young offenders has made it necessary to consider safeguards for the public as well and the Act places both power and responsibility on local authorities to provide secure accommodation. It also raises the age range for control and care of some cases from eighteen to nineteen, and this combined with the clear need for more hostels for young people under twenty one will result in many young adults coming within the purview of the children's service. Because of the lower age of majority they will be adults in a legal as well as a bioliogical sense.

Many difficult decisions will have to be made under the new legislation. Prosecutions of young persons over fourteen for offences will be taken by the police who will also, no doubt, conduct some care proceedings for the whole age range up to seventeen. Most decisions to take court proceedings, however, under the provisions of the Bill, will require that the child care service has been consulted and it will therefore have to express a point of view. If all other resources, including voluntary child care measures, have been considered and none found suitable to meet the case, the child care service will still be concerned. Police prosecutions may even begin to be seen as an indication of the effectiveness or otherwise of the service. Even if cases go to court, there will be few alternatives to the child care service resources if something more than voluntary co-operation of parents is required. Interim treatment measures to be used by courts in conjunction with supervision orders will also be a task for the child care service, although it is likely to work closely with others in provision of suitable arrangements. The youth service, probation officers, voluntary organisations, and others jointly with child care will undertake measures to help the rehabilitation of more satisfactory development of young offenders.

The approach embodied in the new legislation will inevitably raise many difficult questions involving society's standards of behaviour, morals and expectations as well as personal standards of individuals. Social workers trying to answer these questions will require sensitivity to human need, public morale, social mores and community involvement. They will need to reflect carefully but also to act with expedition, and have courage at times to take unpopular decisions, whatever these may be. This aspect of their work is likely to develop their social and community awareness more than at present and differences between the child care service's attitudes and those of the more " sheltered " social work groups could, in these respects, become more marked. The need for more staff in the child care service will again be considerable, and the growing proportion of men, in both field work and residential care, is likely to take a sharp turn upwards. The Bill spoke of 1,500 more workers. These will need complementary administrative, office and other staff. Residential work, so long the Cinderella of all the social services, may well be taken more seriously by local authorities when it is known to be providing care and treatment for young offenders in the midst of local communities instead of in country mansions well hidden away from everyday life. More training, shorter hours, higher staffing ratios will be needed and will tend to alter and improve recruitment potential. Such changes and the provision of short term treatment measures might have the healthy effect of focussing attention on the needs of many adolescents for whom the youth service at present is unable to cater. The border line between the offender and the rest will be much less sharply defined and the results may, in the long term, benefit a much wider group than offenders.

child care and the future

It would be interesting to speculate how a different historical sequence of events concerning *Children in trouble* and the Seebohm Report might have influenced the future of the child care service. Because the implementation of *Children in trouble* has preceded the implementation of Seebohm, the child care service which will face re-organisation on Seebohm lines will be larger and more committed to the care of young offenders than it would otherwise have been. Child care professional evidence to the Seebohm Committee clearly envisaged the service losing its separate identity and being absorbed within a unified social work department. Both before the Committee reported and since, however, the child care service has refused to accept that the department should be a combined health and social work department as some local authorities would like it to be, or that it should be headed by anyone other than a fellow social work professional or a social administrator with social work experience. The arguments on both sides have been rehearsed many times, but, assuming that the major recommendations of Seebohm are implemented by law, and that the health service remains separate and absorbs local as well as regional health services, how will the future of the children's service develop?

A unified social service as now envisaged will require considerable resources of administrative experience, energy and adaptability within its personnel. In comparison with the other personal social service sections likely to be combined within it child care could have a great deal to offer. Administrative experience gained by many child care staff over the last ten years in particular should be valuable in the new service, and in residential work, work with families in their own homes, and in the proportion of staff with professional or allied training in social work, the service will be a major element in any new department. By comparison with others too, it has taken a promotional view of its work and this is likely to mean that many of its former staff will wish to push Seebohm recommendations forward once implementation begins, rather than being willing to hold fire indefinitely as some local authority personnel have grown accustomed to doing in other welfare settings. Other changes the service will have to accept are likely to be necessary whether Seebohm is accepted or shelved. One of the most important is the recognition that social work is something more than casework, and that casework training is only part of a wide range of skills needed by social workers, whether field or residential. The history of the child care service in particular tends to illustrate the way in which social work in general is being pushed by events to make a decision as to whether it continues to be a way of helping people to sort out and put up with intolerable situations with more equanimity than they would otherwise have done, or whether, in addition to that, it must accept the role of a pressure group within society, commenting on intolerable situations and seeking to remedy them by means of national policy as well as individual supportive work. The new legislation on young offenders and the implications of a Seebohm approach could both point child care workers further in this direction. Many are willingly looking that way already. It may in fact be easier for some to accept this than to modify attitudes to casework as a method, although there are encouraging signs that community work, group work, mixed field and residential work are all forming " growing points " in some departments and will act as precedents for others to use and emulate in varied ways.

The future of the child care service cannot be considered apart from its past and present. In whatever setting the needs of children are met, they are not likely to change in basic character, only recognition of problems and methods of help may change, widen and deepen. It is logical that preventive work with families should become part of a service promoting community support and group work and encouraging client participation. Work to prevent juvenile offending and liberalise the community's approach to it could lead to more enlightened attitudes to adult offenders: helping individuals to obtain their " rights " from income supportive services, housing departments and others could result in promotion of " social action." Whether separately or as part of a unified social service, the increasing knowledge and experience the child care service gains of how best to provide all children with a satisfactory childhood, is likely to have wide-reaching implications for all social services and the community in general. It began as a service for a

E

relatively small group of deprived children away from home. In twenty years it has become involved with hundreds of thousands of children in need and trouble in their own homes. Its future must lie with the welfare of all children at risk, whether from poverty, homelessness, emotional need or social inequity.

4. housing : foundations of an effective service ?

Hilary Rose

It is interesting that the Seebohm report titled the section in which housing takes pride of place " Foundations of an effective service." I am happy to accept the premise involved here and to continue the imagery involved, particularly if we pick out another theme—that of resources—which runs throughout the report, as together they explain why we must survey the quality and the quantity of the foundations before we can consider first, the rationalised edifice Seebohm invited us to construct, and second, the actual bill for the reorganisation of the social services presently offered to Parliament.

A check of one of the telling, if rudimentary indices, of the state of the foundations is the level of homelessness. Here despite Milner Holland, Cathy, and Shelter, and despite the existence of a well-permeated Labour government, for the past five years the numbers continue to rise. One hopes that the Labour government has protected the social services and those in greatest need better than the Conservatives would have done in a similar prolonged economic crisis; however, the suspicion that this difference is more metaphysical than real is increasingly gaining credence. CPAG's recent memorandum (*Incomes policy for families*) submitted in January 1970, to the Minister of State for the Social Services, argued that the poor are worse off under Labour, noting record unemployment, massive price increases and the failure of the incomes policy. The most recent homeless figures (1968) stand at 18,849, that is, a rise of over 3,100 people, over and above the previous year (*Ministry of Health annual report*, 1968). Some comfort can perhaps be derived from the possible humanising effects of the triple ministry circular which urged authorities to make provision for fathers to be admitted wherever possible as well as mothers and children; it is also urged that communal living provision for families in temporary accommodation should be upgraded urgently (Ministry of Health 1967, Home Office 177/67, MHLG 20/66).

This has perhaps made it easier for families to turn to the local authorities for accommodation by decreasing their fears of being broken up, and has, at the same time, contributed to this increase. However, it would be unwise to derive too much comfort and to assume that even this figure reflects the full incidence of the most acute form of housing distress, as there are some critical rationing barriers for the would-be officially homeless family to cross. First there is the relative humanity of bloody mindedness of differing local authorities. The Seebohm report also makes this point but with rather more tactful nomenclature, it distinguishes between the " helpful " and the " unhelpful " authorities.

I remember one quite senior welfare officer explaining seriously, to me, that " in the thirties we had the problem of the workshy, now we have the problem of the homeshy." Secondly we have the not immediately explicable discrepancy between the number of applications for temporary accommodation and the number of admissions. Within the Greater London area, which accounts for over half the admissions and where by and large a liberal attitude prevails, applications run at rather more than threefold the admissions.

There is also reason to suspect that the continuing increase in the number of the homeless (2,500 up in 1967, 3,100 up in 1968) may partly be caused by the attitude of the Supplementary Benefits Commission which is refusing to recognise as " reasonable " local authority rents that, by some curious twist of logic, it is " reasonable " to expect the tenant to pay by finding the £9 or £10 a week demanded.

new homes

Nor for that matter, despite the widespread publicity given to the target of half a million houses per year—briefly reached in 1965 when we pushed up our building rate to 7.0 new houses per thousand population—have we been able to maintain this target. The original proposal was that new housebuilding be constructed equally by the local authority and the owner-occupier sectors, but even at the current, reduced targets there is evidence that the local authorities are not going to be able to maintain their share. Nor can we assume that this much adjusted new target will necessarily produce houses for those experiencing the most acute housing stress. The shockingly low productivity of some authorities, such as those in West London, renders invalid the defence of this low target which some government apologists have put forward. And if we examine international statistics neither our housebuilding rate, nor our level of investment in housing compare anything other than individously with countries of similar wealth and size (*Annual bulletin of housing and building statistics for Europe,* UN Economic Commission for Europe). We are neither adding to the housing stock sufficiently fast, nor caring for the existing stock adequately. The government survey in *Old houses into new homes,* reported in 1968 that no less than 6.3 millions (40 per cent) of the total stock of 15.7 million dwellings are either unfit or in need of substantial repairs (Cmnd 3602, HMSO 1968). It was recognised in this White Paper and the ensuing Bill that, for the most part, these are in the privately rented sector and located in areas of environmental poverty, and an area approach was proposed. Nonetheless the fact remains that the number of actual improvement grants taken up in the last year is lower than it was seven years ago and that, of these grants, only a fifth have been utilised by private landlords.

private landlords

Yet it is the private landlord, as John Greve's study of the London homeless (John Greve *London's homeless,* Bell 1964) John Rex's study of Birmingham (John Rex and Robert Moore *Race, Community and conflict,* OUP 1966) and the Milner Holland

Report (*Report of the committee on housing in Greater London*, Cmnd 2605, 1965) all make distressingly apparent, who continues to shelter the urban poor. The condition of these, the large families of the unskilled, the elderly, the fatherless families, the newcomers, especially the non-white newcomers, are what the social service view of housing is all about. That is a view of housing as a right. I am conscious that it is not my brief but that of Tony Lynes to discuss welfare rights, but it would appear from events, such as those of squatter families moving into unoccupied houses that there are embryonic signs that some of the poor are beginning to believe that housing is a right too. Indeed it seems despite the frailty of the movement, that the squatters have made a positive contribution towards the prevention of homelessness in that local authorities have been forced to re-examine their policies of leaving property empty pending redevelopment and reallocation. There is a tinge of irony in the fact that last time there was a squatters' movement which became quite powerful, there was also a Labour government. Thus it appears that the double message of Milner Holland—to improve the quality and security of privately rented housing, and to hold the size of the privately rented sector against its steady erosion to owner-occupation—has been only very partially heard. So far the changes in the rent structure achieved through the fair-rent procedures set up on the basis of the Milner Holland report have tended to establish rents of about £6 per week on average, which is well above the rent paying ability of the average working class family. Not very surprisingly, this has generated a good deal of hostility to this scheme, which is not easily assuaged. Even the argument put forward by David Donnison ("How to help the poorest tenants?" *New Society*, 16 January 1969) that the Act is not working too badly as, although only a minority (35 per cent) of the cases have resulted in reduced rents, these are the poorest tenancies and the poorest tenants, the evidence, such as that afforded by Michael Zander's Islington Study (*New Society*, 12 September 1968) that the poorest and weakest tenants are the *least* likely to go to either rent officers or rent tribunals and secure what legal rights they have, additionally reduces our sense of confidence in the fair-rent procedures. In this situation there remains an urgent need for a public authority to take over the management and maintenance of what private rented property remains, in the most stressed areas. This technique, particularly if the faint shadow of municipalisation which lies within it were to be encouraged, could both plug the loss of this housing type and also improve the quality. At present we are failing to do either on a scale commensurate with housing need.

I have not discussed Seebohm's interim arrangements—the quota system, whereby a percentage of houses are earmarked for the Social Service Department— because I think this presses on the crucial dilemma of housing. This dilemma is that housing is charged with two not really compatible functions. At least they are not really compatible in a situation of continuing shortage. One function is as a utility for the working classes, that is, providing decent housing at a reasonable rent; the other is the social service function, where housing serves those most in need first. At present the waiting lists are lengthening. In London the average wait is about sixteen years: unless one is sufficiently fortunate to be in a slum-clearance or road scheme, or to acquire tuberculosis. At the same time racial hostility is growing, scarcely allayed by the Government's record on immigration; nor does the record of the Race Relations Board and Commission inspire undue confidence for the future. Unmarried mothers and large problem families are also not particularly kindly regarded. It is relatively easy to be liberal from the privacy and comfort of an owner-occupied home. For the working class the choice is more brutal. It's "them," in some sense the social deviants, or " us," the ordinary working man and his family, that are housed. The price for such an approach, which emphasises ingenious administrative devices for allocating scarce resources to the most needy, may well feed the antagonisms which divide our society and effectively inhibit the co-operative values which, without a programme stressing community care, lives dangerously near to rhetoric. At the grass roots level in the local authorities this dilemma is often understood with painful clarity. As a second welfare officer explained to me, " The purpose of case-work with a multi-problem family in or out of a recuperative unit is to restore them to normal functioning, that is, to enable them to take their turn on the waiting list." There is, as Seebohm says, a problem of resources, right at the foundation level.

The present Bill reflects Seebohm's basic weakness, which was to accept the resource limitation argument far too easily and, therefore, implicitly establish a self-fulfilling prophecy, it is crucial that we look carefully at the functions of the new Social Service Department. This is particularly so in the case of responsibility for the accommodation of homeless families, which was to have become a Housing Department responsibility and under the Bill appears to remain with the Social Service Department. This must be changed, as it offers at least the diminution and at best the prevention of homelessness through local authority evictions, which are a not insubstantial percentage of the total of homeless families. But, by and large, the question which has to be asked, whether of the Report itself or the organisational reform it has engendered, is—who is it supposed to serve? Already I have suggested that the Report was designed to serve the social work profession. The Bill seems to be designed to promote the power of the central departments, without even the virtue of clarity in positing exactly which central department it means. At no point in the Bill is it clear just which Secretary of State, whether Health and Social Security or the Home Office, is responsible for which functions. We are left with a hope that public debate in and out of the House will force Ministers to make a public decision as to their responsibilities. It has often been housing in general and the homeless in particular who have borne the brunt of inter-departmental and central and local government confusion of responsibility. For example, it was necessary to involve three Ministers to secure a circular to modify the authoritarian and inhumane management of much part three accommodation. If the major goal of the Seebohm Bill is a more rational administrative structure for the social services, then it is more than time that some of these problems were resolved—if only for the simple reason that we should know to whom we should address our complaints!

no coherent strategy

These then are some of the indications that the foundations are insecure. What we have seen is not so much the art of papering over the cracks with legislation, it is more like trying to build a house with *papier maché*. If we ask why the foundations are in this condition, the answer must lie in the fact that there has been no coherent strategy to enable us to unravel the labyrinthine complexity of the housing subsidies (John Greve " Housing policies and prospects " *Political Quarterly,* January-March, 1969) which came in various guises, including tax allowances, local authority subsidies, rent rebates, rent controls, supplementary benefits, and rate rebates, all directed to making housing cheaper for some group or another. Despite some abortive skirmishing with the tax allowance arrangements, there has been no target date announced to limit the tax allowance available on mortgage interest for the well-to-do owner occupiers. Nor, as John Greve has pointed out recently (*op cit*) has there been any attempt to deal with the chronic burden of housing authorities who built at low rates of interest and must now pay back at increasingly dear rates, so that as much as 70 per cent of the housing account is devoted to merely servicing the loan. Equally, although the long awaited reforms of local government are now in sight, for too long we have suffered the impossibility of changing some 1,500 motley bodies with the responsibility for the whole of the housing programme. including the massive task of urban renewal which now confronts us. When we recall that Aneurin Bevan's original refusal to push the municipalisation programme was explicitly based on this self-same impossibility, and we see that the number of post-Maud bodies is to be reduced, then the possibility of resolving the problems of privately rented housing comes into sight.

It is not as if what has been said here is new; the outlines of strategy have been clear for some time. Nor for that matter are the names of Cullingworth, Donnison, Glass, Greve, Nevitt, Parker and Rex unknown; (five out of the seven are Fabian authors, and at least four advise or act as consultants to the government) the problem is that this Government is in its sixth year and has not moved from pragmatism to planning.

If we accept the fragmented and untidy nature of Seebohm's foundations, is it possible to examine the administrative proposals to see whether they afford any immediate help, and whether they help or hinder any future rationalisation of housing itself? In some sense the question has to be ducked, because it is far from clear that either Seebohm or the Green Papers—either Mark I or Mark II— can be described as manifestoes of a new concept of the social services. Their chief proposals are to co-ordinate the personal social services within one department and to integrate the tripartite structure of health in Mark I (*The administrative structure of the medical and related services in England and Wales,* Ministry of Health, 1968) under the area board and in Mark II (*The future of the National Health Service,* DHSS, 1970) under a two-tier arrangement, parallel with the post-Maud structure of local government. Nonetheless these changes are for the most part rationalisation of existing trends and policies, with little major stock-taking to see if the trends are themselves right. Thus, the Seebohm Report gives us an interesting chapter on consumer involvement in the social services, but fails to think through the problem of participation. It does not in its own work, even through that somewhat remote method of consultation—the social survey, ask the consumers of existing social services what they want from any future structure. Thus, the report defers to the consumers verbally, but in substance addresses itself almost exclusively to the administrative problems of the social work profession. Indeed, when we examine the Bill which has resulted from Seebohm, even this verbal deference is removed and we are faced with straightforward bureaucratic rationalisation. Nowhere does the Report or the Bill embrace a new concept of community care with participation, which would encourage, if not ensure, more spending on such crucial services as home helps and hostel accommodation. Seebohm's very modesty concerning the need to do what we can with present resources reflects more temperance than vision, yet I suspect that it is the latter which is needed to shift the level of spending on the social services to a new level.

Yet one of the modest gains from this temperate spirit was reflected in Seebohm's proposals for the new housing department, which was to be expanded to take in all housing functions, leaving only the recuperative units for rehabilitation work with multi-problem families as a social service responsiblity. Thus, the Seebohm housing department was to be responsible for the main housing programme, together with special and sheltered housing, and temporary accommodation for the homeless. In principle this looked a sound move placing the responsibility for those whose sole problem is housing with a housing department. The added advantage of a social service department losing its problems of housing management should also have enabled it to concentrate on social service functions.

Seebohm's case for " special housing," to take the earliest proposals first, is in many ways a negative case which has emerged because of the long history of the demographic irrelevance of much of the local authority building programme, which has been desperately slow to respond to the need to build either small dwellings for the old or large dwellings for the big families. For too long there has been a virtually immutable law of the two/three bedroomed house. The new enlarged housing departments which are likely to emerge from the restructuring of local government, given even relatively modest research and intelligence services, should be able to manage to build, adapt, exchange housing to aid either elderly or handicapped people. Essentially the existing arrangements could be speeded up and improved, but retained as a need sensitive function within housing.

The case for locating the chief responsibility for sheltered housing within the Housing Department is much weaker. First its role seems to be much more analagous to that of the recuperative units, which Seebohm does propose to allocate to the Social Service Department, than the committee is prepared to recognise. One wonders if the medico-social element present in sheltered housing stirred the breasts of the committee less effectively than the casework element present in recuperative unit work, when half the committee were members or associated with the National Institute of Social Work Training. But more serious than a mere anomaly is the criticism that, because of the cost per unit of each sheltered dwelling —each group requiring a warden—the housing department is likely to regard the resources spent as being only modestly productive. In this case the kinds of pressures developed by placing sheltered housing in the department would have similarities to those created by the existing arrangements involving two tiers of local government, pressures which have led to a very modest number of sheltered dwellings being built. Even by 1971 the target is for only 159,000. Thus, if the housing department becomes the prime department for this responsibility, the economic pressures are likely to be against community care and towards institutionalisation, which is the antithesis of Seebohm's goals.

Certain objections can be raised. The most serious is the risk of the emergence of a different and second class type of housing. This would be a valid objection were special housing to be included, but limited to sheltered housing the relatively small scale of the operation fails to make this a real threat. Co-operation in design and management will, as Seebohm rightly points out, be necessary. But the determination to keep people in the community will come from the Social Service Department, as it ties in both with its growing commitment to community care, and also, not unimportantly, the sheer financial constraints and manpower shortage associated with the provision of homes.

5. the community mental health sevices

Peter Mittler

Eleven years after the Mental Health Act, and seven years after the first Health and Welfare Plan, how effective are our community mental health services, and what should our priorities be?

The achievements are certainly impressive, by the standards of eleven years ago, and by the standards of many other countries today, and it is no wonder that some of our ministerial spokesmen sometimes sound complacent. I shall not review the achievements and shortcomings of the service here, since the ground was covered in two previous Fabian pamphlets (Peter Mittler, *The mental health services*, Fabian research series 252 and *Mental health services in the community*, Fabian occasional paper 4), but concentrate instead on the theme of quality rather than quantity, and consider a number of ways in which quality might be improved, not necessarily at prohibitive cost.

" One of the main discoveries (or a rediscovery) of modern psychiatry is the profound influence that the social environment has on the well being and level of functioning of people with any kind of mental disorder." This opening sentence from the Seebohm chapter on mental health services is really the crux of the whole problem of planning effective social services for the mentally disordered. But though Seebohm rightly highlighted the influence of the social environment, he failed to spell out in detail the way in which these influences work for good and ill; more documentation of this theme might have been helpful—such as on institutional neurosis, research on families of schizophrenics, the nature of the burden carried by families of different types of patient, and the ways in which social problems have already been tackled in some areas.

There are several points at which the services and resources might be brought to bear more directly on the treatment and welfare of the patient, and these will be briefly outlined below.

linking hospitals and the community

Seebohm reminded us that hospitals are in the community, but there is evidence that the links between them are often tenuous. Our concern with community care has distracted attention from the hospitals, at least until there are disturbing reports of neglect, cruelty and deprivation, or until a serious fire reveals a desperate shortage of staff. Neither the public nor the professions not immediately involved are aware of the conditions in which some patients still have to live, and in which staff have to work.

The staff are more aware than anyone of the deficiencies of the service, and far from bereft of ideas on how the situation could be improved, but they tend to appear before the public as defenders of their institutions against what they regard as irresponsible and ill-informed criticism by the press and others.

One way of bridging the gulf between hospital and the community is through voluntary workers. Some hospitals have begun to do this by recruiting a paid organiser to increase and co-ordinate the number of voluntary helpers, of whom there are probably a substantial number in the community, willing and interested in helping patients to establish some kind of link with the outside world. Loss of contact with people outside the hospital is, of course, one of the worst deprivations suffered by the long term psychiatric patient, and one which renders his rehabilitation difficult. The shortage of nurses makes it difficult in most wards to do more than keep the ward running, but the influx of voluntary workers from the community could do much to infuse some elements of normality into the routine of institutional life. But these voluntary workers must receive systematic briefing and guidance in what to do and what to expect. They must be prepared to learn something about mental illness and the part they can usefully play, otherwise their presence on the ward may do more harm than good, and only result in suspicion and hostility from the staff. The job of the organiser is to make the task easier both for the staff, the volunteers and hence for the patients.

Perhaps the most pressing need, and certainly the easiest to fill, is for volunteers to come regularly into hospitals for the subnormal, particularly to play with the children. A recent survey of 34 hospitals revealed that only one ward had any books or toys, and another had a box of paints (G. A. Bland, *Education in hospital schools for the mentally handicapped*, College of Special Education, 1968). In many hospitals, a single nurse has to cope with up to 50 children; half of them do not go to the hospital school, and are on the ward all day, with little to do, and very rarely any activities. (P. Morris, *Put Away*, Routledge, 1969). Mentally subnormal children can be greatly helped by properly thought out and guided play experiences, and volunteers seem well suited for this task. Many of them will have children of their own, but even so will need advice from experienced people—mainly teachers and psychologists—on the play needs of handicapped children. There is now a good deal of thought on the best means of bringing play experiences to severely handicapped or bedfast children, and the Council for Children's Play is active in this field.

A similar development which is already under way is for girls from secondary schools to spend part of their school day in junior training schools, helping to play with and stimulate severely handicapped children who need individual attention. The teacher, even in a class of five or six children, cannot work very long with the individual child, but can often delegate a particular task to a young and otherwise inexperienced helper. In this way both may benefit from the experience; in the last analysis, community care depends on the tolerance, understanding and, above all, knowledge that we can pass on to the next generation about the nature of handicaps and the ordinary needs of children for play and normal experiences which they are unable to seek out for themselves.

help for families

The suggestion for a more active involvement of the community in the work of hospitals is only one way of helping hospital staff to infuse more of a spirit of normality into what are often dismal and depressing surroundings. But community care depends above all on the quality of the help that is given to families of the mentally disordered, and here the service is still lamentably weak.

Families are given very little help in the problems presented by having a handicapped person in their midst, though it is true that the resourcefulness and resilience of many of them are remarkable. If, under the banner of community care, we are going to have more handicapped people continuing to live at home, then we must be prepared to offer more guidance and more practical help to families. In the first place, an allowance should be paid to families for looking after a handicapped relative, as is the case in the Scandinavian countries. Secondly, home help, home nursing and laundering facilities should be available to those who need them, together with " babysitting " and similar services from time to time so that parents can occasionally go out together. The hardships suffered by parents of mentally handicapped children have been documented for some years, and there is no need for a government survey lasting several more years to establish the need (J. Tizard and J. C. Grad, *The mentally handicapped and their families*, Oxford University Press, 1961).

Finally, adults who are disabled from birth should have a right to a disability pension under the new pension proposals, in the same way as those who are disabled in industry or in the armed forces, and not as a supplementary benefit. Poverty, poor housing, and lack of occupation are often the price that the handicapped pay for the benefits of remaining in the community. All too often the subnormal adult is admitted to hospital when his family can no longer look after him, although he has virtually no need of the nursing or medical services of the hospital—merely for its " asylum."

Families also need much more skilled and informed advice on practical problems involved in having a handicapped relative in the family. Mothers of subnormal children receive virtually no advice at present on how to help their child through play, how to widen his experiences and enlarge his understanding of the world. After the initial diagnosis, she has to wait until her child is five or older before he again comes into skilled care, but even then she is cut off from advice herself, even though her child may be receiving more attention. Similarly, much more could be done to prepare families in detail for the problems they are likely to encounter in helping a relative with a psychiatric illness. Psychiatrists do what they can, but their time is limited, and community care should make more provision for this kind of consultative help to be available through the local mental health services.

training

All this and much more depends on a trained staff, and this is all too obvious a weakness of community care at present. Despite a great increase in the number of training courses for social workers and others involved in mental health services, only about half of all local authority social workers will be qualified in the mid-1970s, and probably for some time beyond. Mental welfare officers, who carry most of the day to day work of the mental health services, have few training courses specifically for their needs, and very few of them have any formal training for their work, though many have had a great deal of relevant experience in mental nursing or teaching of the subnormal. In many parts of the country they are not involved in a " teaching " relationship with psychiatrists, and their contact with specialists is all too limited. Nevertheless, they are expected to help in the rehabilitation and occupation of patients discharged from hospitals, and to give support and guidance to their families. They work against heavy odds, at low pay, and with little professional help. Their task will not be made easier without more training and more recognition of their key role in community care.

Not only do we need to increase the number of trained staff, but we need a reappraisal of the kind of training courses provided. For example, short, intensive courses of training, say 3 months, or a course of evening sessions, is better than nothing at all, and a course of formal lectures on, say, the nature of schizophrenia, may be less valuable than a series of guided seminars or " mock " (or live) case conferences. The abolition of the divisions between the local health authorities and the regional hospital boards may make it possible for area health boards to think seriously about organising really effective in-service training for domiciliary staff, not only social workers but health visitors and others, including voluntary workers. Even the universities might play a more active role in organising training courses for the staff of community services. Refresher courses are, of course, also essential.

Much could be done to improve the service by a more flexible attitude to the employment of part-time workers. There are real difficulties in the allocation of duties, but these can be overcome; in nursing and teaching, for example, more women are being employed on a part-time basis. More guidance from central government might well do something to encourage the more backward local authorities.

central guidance and inspection

The nettle of central guidance and control has to be firmly grasped. We have had many years of local autonomy, and the result is that some parts of the country are years ahead of others in the quantity and quality of their mental health services. All this is in the sacred British tradition of the autonomy of the local authority. In the mental health field, there is the additional complication of not only being unwilling to tell the local authority what to do, but of appearing to interfere with the clinical freedom of a doctor in treating his patients. Anyone who has sat on a Ministry of Health committee will have been impressed by the often radical and original thinking of Ministry doctors and officials, but at the same time dismayed at the judicious tone of their communications with local health authorities. The forewords to the various Health and Welfare revisions are only the published examples. Clinical freedom is a myth at a time when the government forbids hospitals to replace nurses who leave the service or makes constant cuts in essential services. It seems only logical to take the next step and ensure that every local health authority and hospital maintains minimum standards and provides an effective service. One way to bring about some improvement is to appoint an inspectorate for our mental health services. The case for an inspectorate is undeniable in any institution that looks after children, since to deny to subnormal children the facilities and overall control that have long been available to normal children is negative discrimination indeed. We need an educational inspectorate to ensure that subnormal children, both in hospitals and junior training centres, receive education suited to their needs, and to see that the schools are run along appropriate educational lines. An inspecorate is even more badly needed, however, to ensure that conditions on hospital wards provide a reasonably active and stimulating environment, and that the children have a good supply of suitable toys, and are played with by the staff. An inspectorate is also needed in all psychiatric hospitals and units in order to ensure that reasonable standards of physical care and welfare are provided for all the patients, and to help the staff to secure better treatment facilities. Such a policy seems neither autocratic nor inhuman, provided the inspectorate is carefully chosen, and their work results in a real improvement in conditions, though obviously there will be difficulties in defining their responsibilities and powers.

conclusions

Community care for the mentally disordered is a fine slogan and a splendid goal, but we are not yet within sight of it. Local authorities have vastly increased their expenditure, a lot of buildings have been put up, and many improvements made to services. But there is always the danger of the patient passing from skilled to un-skilled care, in the sloppy and sentimental belief that it is always better for people to remain in the community and to be kept out of hospitals. Whether or not this is true as a generalisation depends, amongst other things, on the quality of care provided both in the hospital and in the community. The hospital can work usefully in the community (many have done so successfully for years) and the community can also become more actively involved in the hospital, both through professional work and through guided voluntary workers. But help for families, whether we call it casework or practical, is surely an essential of community care, and it is in this respect that the service is still deficient.

The time is ripe for study, research and reappraisal of what community care now involves, and what its achievements might be in the future. No amount of co-ordination of services can make up for a lack of ideas, no amount of good will compensate for a lack of appreciation that mental disorders call for skilled and informed treatment.

6. the old: the future of community care

Michael Meacher

" Anything which makes the elderly a race apart, whether special residential areas or special clubs and associations, puts them in a sort of zoo or ante-chamber of death." (*Preparation for retirement*, Yorkshire Council of Social Service, 1966). Not the least problem in preparing plans to realise the potential of community services for the aged lies in persuading doctors and the general public that old people can still sustain various valuable roles, that much infirmity and social misery is remediable or at least preventable, and above all that it is worth the time, energy and cost to arrange remedy or prevention. Widespread acceptance of non-resuscitation after cardiac arrest of persons over 65, if not of euthanasia itself, reveals a dispirited public response. Even courses for retirement, which have recently proliferated, sometimes stress negative aspects, for instance " how to manage on a reduced income " or, inadvertently, the vacuousness of leisure in the absence of function, and the emphasis is normally on decline or " desocialisation," to use René König's numbing phrase.

A rational policy, however, uninhibited by current forebodings about the growing " burden " of old age based on the (incorrect) belief that elderly people nowadays live longer, must start from the present health and welfare needs of old people living in the community as elucidated by research. Secondly, it must estimate the degree of need unmet by particular services, with reference to both the inadequacy of coverage, deficiencies of quality and the demand for hitherto untried services. Thirdly, it should consider the extent of needs unmet by particular local authorities, the degree of variation in provision unexplained by variation in needs, the question of the possible substitutability of services, and the role of central government in raising standards and reducing the uneven distribution of local services. A fourth aim of policy should be to examine the reasons for the persistence of such an enormity of unmet need, together with measures to make consumer demand more effective. The main considerations here embrace both the principle of self-application underlying the distribution of services and the resignation of old people towards disabilities as inevitable concomitants of age, plus their fear of applying because of the reflection on their loss of independence. Fifthly, in this light future policy must select as its central target the development of effective techniques of primary and secondary prevention. At the immediate level, a policy of seeking-out demand rather than waiting for opting-in would require regular visiting of all persons of retirement age, together with special priority for members of known " risk " groups, and the implementation of a more effective system of co-ordination and psycho-geriatric assessment. At a more anticipatory level, the preservation of economic and social roles as a defence against deterioration and to sustain self-determination would require both a more resolute effort to extend employment opportunities for older workers and a more positive attempt to keep the extended family intact to permit, wherever possible, an interchange of services. Lastly, the costing of domiciliary as opposed to residential care should be examined, and the implications of these policies considered in terms of a shift in public expenditure towards preventive services. Above all, a technique should be evolved by government for the redeployment of the present unequal distribution of resources towards those areas in greatest need, as revealed by risk registers. Each of these items of policy will now be explored in turn.

unmet needs of old people in the community

Several local studies of the last twenty years have drawn attention to the vast extent of disability, much of it remediable, among old people living in private households. The most comprehensive survey of their unmet health needs has been that undertaken among a random sample of the population aged 65 and over in three general practices in and around Edinburgh. (J. Williamson, I. H. Stokoe, *et al*, " Old people at home: their unreported needs," *The Lancet*, 23 May 1964). If their findings are representative of the national picture, then the incidence of medical disabilities and mental disorders among the old unrecognised by doctors must approximate to the pattern revealed in the tables below. These figures show a massive amount of morbidity at present untreated, and a large degree of unmet need for various welfare services. The effect of these figures is all the more startling in view of the known fact that disabilities in old age tend to be multiple rather than single. A study of

ESTIMATED INCIDENCE OF UNRECOGNISED MEDICAL NEEDS AMONG OLD PEOPLE, AGED 65 AND OVER, IN BRITAIN, 1962.

medical need	number
feet disabilities	2,184,000
locomotor disease (commonly osteoarthritis of knee and hip joints, but excluding feet)	932,000
visual defects	1,252,000
hearing defects	1,340,000
lack of dentures*	990,000
varicose veins	845,000
respiratory disorders (including chronic bronchitis)	320,000
alimentary disorders	466,000
genito-urinary disease	903,000
heart disease	379,000
anaemia (haemoglobin 80% or less)	408,000
diabetes	6,000
arteriosclerosis	1,777,000
diseases of the central nervous system	175,000
total elderly population in private households	5,825,000

*A. Greenlees and J. Adams, *Old people in Sheffield*, 1950

ESTIMATED INCIDENCE OF MENTAL DISORDER AMONG OLD PEOPLE, AGED 65 AND OVER, IN BRITAIN, 1962.

mental disorder	number
dementia	1,398,000
neurotic disorder	583,000
depression	466,000

200 patients admitted to a geriatric unit in Aberdeen found that the men had a mean of 6.4 disorders each and the women 5.4 each (L. A. Wilson, I. R. Lawson and W. Brass, " Multiple disorders in the elderly," *The Lancet*, 27 October 1962). This simple classification does not, of course, exhaust the needs of old people living in the community. Other needs no less important interlock with those already mentioned, including lack of money, lack of companionship or affection, lack of adequate nutrition and lack of occupation. We know, for example, that $1\frac{3}{4}$ million men and women aged 65 and over had total incomes of less than £4 a week when national assistance scale rates plus rent allowances stood at an average £3 15s 0d for a single householder (P. Townsend and D. Wedderburn, *The aged in the welfare state*, p 88, Bell, 1965) and that 850,000 pensioners in 1965 had incomes low enough to entitle them to assistance, though they were not receiving it (Ministry of Pensions and National Insurance, *Financial and other circumstances of retirement pensioners*, HMSO, 1966).

We know that approximately 1 million old people have sufficiently few social contacts to be termed isolated, and that in overlapping but not identical categories 1.6 million are afflicted by loneliness and another 1 million experience a severe

ESTIMATED NEED FOR WELFARE AND HOUSING SERVICES AMONG OLD PEOPLE, AGED 65 AND OVER, IN BRITAIN, 1962.

welfare and housing services	number
home help: both those feeling a need for help and those having difficulty with housework and having no help	600,000
mobile meals: those wanting hot meals	344,000
those lacking three basic housing amenities (indoor WC and sole use of bath and kitchen)	355,000
those lacking 2 of the 3 basic housing amenities	1,281,000
those incapacitated and living alone and also with no children within a 10 minute journey	297,000
laundry: those requiring laundry services*	874,000

*C. Gordon, J. G. Thomson and I. R. Emerson, *Medical Officer*, 98, 1957, 19.
source: P. Townsend and D. Wedderburn, *The aged in the welfare state*, p 69, Bell, 1965.

feeling of hopelessness or personal disorganisation, while 1.3 million live alone (J. Tunstall, *Old and alone*, p 1, Routledge, 1966). We know too that the vulnerability of old people is enhanced by the greater prevalence of malnutrition at the higher ages. One study found that 41 per cent of old people admitted to hospital were deficient in ascorbic acid and 59 per cent deficient in vitamin B1, while among the elderly at home who were not ill 27 per cent were deficient in vitamin C and 22 per cent in vitamin B1 (L. L. Griffiths, J. C. Brocklehurst, *et al*, *British Medical Journal*, 19 March 1966). Also we know that work and the comradeship of fellow workers is missed by perhaps a quarter of men in old age, whilst as many as 39 per cent of recently retired men in Britain would like to return to work (E. Shanas, P. Townsend, *et al*, *Old people in three industrial societies*, p 338, Routledge). But crucial though these other aspects of need are, attention will be concentrated, in the limited space available, on requirements for the health and welfare services.

EXPECTED PERCENTAGE INCREASES IN THE POPULATION OF ENGLAND AND WALES AGED 65 AND OVER BETWEEN 1961 AND 2001.

year	65-74		75-84		85+	
	male	female	male	female	male	female
1961*	1,419	2,102	594	1,081	90	212
	100	100	100	100	100	100
1971	125	115	104	117	112	137
1981	137	124	132	138	117	163
1991	138	110	146	151	154	200
2001	134	111	150	140	168	223

*actual figures in thousands.
source: Registrar General's *Statistical review of England and Wales for* 1966, part II, p 8.

Even this formidable catalogue of need, however, fails to reveal to the full extent the absolute level of demand which will face future services. The table above indicates that we can expect a sharp increase at least until 1981 in the numbers of the elderly population in the first decade of retirement, so that by 1991 those in the second decade (aged 75-84) will have increased by half over the present levels and those 85 and over will have doubled in number to a total approaching two-thirds of a million. These are certainly substantial increases, but they do not give cause for immediate despair. The index of dependency, based on the ratio of non-productive members of society to the productive, may be scarcely higher in 1981 (estimated at 1.24:1) than in 1951 (1.23:1), and may be actually lower in 2001 when it is estimated at 1.22:1 (B. Benjamin, *Demographic influences on the demand for social services*, unpublished paper, 1967). What these figures do unequivocally show, since morbidity rates and welfare needs rise sharply among the older age groups within the elderly population, is the necessity to pre-empt a disproportionate amount of future resources for the domiciliary care of the aged.

extent of needs unmet by particular services

Estimating the extent of need unsatisfied by particular services raises many hazardous problems, largely because old people are often diffident about acknowledging what external observers might recognise as need. However, the substantial measure of agreement between a variety of independent surveys on this subject reduces the likelihood that such external judgments are unreasonably arbitrary. First, several studies suggest that many more old people require existing services than are receiving them. On the basis that a conservative 20 per cent of the aged needed chiropody, and that an average of six treatments per year would be required, it has been calculated that a seven-fold increase is necessary in the number of old people covered by this key preventive service and a nine-fold increase in the number of treatments (G. Gibson, *New Society*, 13 August 1964). With regard to the mobile meals service, there is evidence that nearly six times more old people would like to have meals brought than actually receive them (P. Townsend and D. Wedderburn, *op cit,* p 49). The latest figures collected from local authorities in 1967 indicate that the proportion of old people supplied has risen from 1.13 per cent in 1962 to nearly 1.7 per cent, but this is still very far short of the 7.0 per cent who have declared their wish to be served with meals. Again, the home help service has been shown to require almost quadrupling in some areas (A. Harris, *Social welfare for the elderly,* vol I, p 66, HMSO, 1968). And in the vitally important field of housing where Peter Townsend has carefully estimated that perhaps 5.1 per cent of old people need sheltered accommodation, the provision of 10.9 special housing units per 1,000 population over 65 by March 1965 (*Health and welfare: the development of community care,* second revision, p 18, cmnd 3022, HMSO 1966) indicates that a five-fold increase in building may be in order. Other services too reveal a similar picture of shortfall of provision.

Not only do very many more people need particular services than receive them, but existing recipients often express a wish for an extension of the service. One study found that 62 per cent of recipients of mobile meals wanted extra meals; included among these were those who already received four meals per week, 63 per cent of whom wanted a further three (S. Harris, *Meals on wheels for old people,* National Corporation for the Care of Old People, table 54, 1960). Again the home help service should be greatly expanded even for those already served by it. A study in Fulham, for example, revealed that district nurses had to prepare meals, carry in the coal and wash up for old people who lived alone on those days when no home help called, especially at weekends, when their presence was solely due to the need to administer injections (S. Sainsbury, *New Society*, 2 April 1964).

With regard to the frequency of medical care, though the great majority of old people seem satisfied that they see their doctor enough, 3.5 per cent of those living at home felt they did not (P. Townsend and D. Wedderburn, *op cit*, p 62). Also existing recipients not only want more of the services they already have, but other services as well. Of those receiving home help, meals and chiropody services, for example, less than 1 per cent were assisted by all three, 9.7 per cent by two, and almost nine-tenths by only one (P. Townsend and D. Wedderburn, *op cit*, p 68).

Nor are the scarce resources available distributed exclusively to those in greatest need. It is known, for instance, that 29 per cent of non-recipients of domiciliary services are incapacitated, including 7 per cent severely so, and 31 per cent also have no relatives living within 10 minutes' journey (P. Townsend and D. Wedderburn, *op cit*, p 30-1). The lack of consultation between the producers of services can yield unfortunate results in terms of priorities. Thus the Fulham study, for example, found that because a meals on wheels scheme run by the local council was not co-ordinated with invalid meals organised by the then LCC, an 80 year old chairbound woman was brought dinners twice a week at 10.30 am, while an active 80 year old woman, with slightly impaired visual judgment, received invalid meals five days a week.

Altogether the picture presented by this data is one of huge deficiency in quantity of provision. How far are local authorities seeking to bridge this gap? The figures are not encouraging. Unfortunately the revised community care plans give only very fragmentary information, and reveal a planned average national rate of increase in certain services not remotely comparable to that required to meet the shortage. For the decade after 1965 local authorities are intending to raise the number of health visitors by only 54 per cent, of home helps (whole-time equivalents) by 48 per cent, and of home nurses by a mere 27 per cent. Even these modest rates of expansion may prove over-optimistic in the light of failures to meet targets already set only two years before. Places in residential homes, on the other hand, are expected to rise by 67 per cent, thus perpetuating, if not reinforcing, the imbalance between institutional and domiciliary care. The only area within the community services for the aged where a more realistic rate of development is planned, in terms of the level of need, lies in the capital building programmes. Special housing over the 6 year period to 1971 is to receive a 151 per cent increase, and centres for the elderly a 273 per cent increase, though the Ministry is strangely reticent about the precise role of the latter, merely remarking cryptically that this trend " no doubt reflects a revision in the light of growing experience of the nature and proper function of a centre properly so-called " (*Health and welfare, op cit*, p 18). Such pusillanimous euphemisms reflect rather the limitations of simply amalgamating local projections than the careful judgments of a real plan. But what is more disquieting still is that the rate of growth anticipated in the personal services in the second half of the decade is scarcely half that of the first, and barely enough even to keep pace with the increase in the oldest age groups (75 and over) who will make the greatest demands on these services.

Examination of the quality of domiciliary services does not offer a much happier impression than the question of sheer coverage. The subject has certainly not yet been adequately investigated, but a limited amount of data suggests that it would repay much closer study. Visiting and clubs are only the most obvious examples where drastic improvements are called for. A study of a voluntary visiting scheme organised by Hornchurch Old People's Welfare Committee revealed that only a fifth of the visitors called at least once a week and spent an hour with the old person, and whilst half of those visited reacted positively, a seventh nursed undisguised antipathy towards what they saw as their visitors' patronising manner (S. Baran, *New Society*, 25 February 1965). Several surveys have shown that visitors are often unable to handle the problems presented to them. However in only a quarter of local authority visiting schemes are records kept of people visited and visitors encouraged to call in other agencies where necessary (G. Gibson *New Society*, 20 August 1964). But perhaps the most serious drawback in this field is the very high turnover of visitors, with devastating consequences where substitutes are not found, as the Fulham study illustrated. An 81 year old woman " had found an ideal visitor in a young woman training for social work. Unfortunately, once her training was over, the student was never replaced, and the widow now found her afternoons interminable."

Social clubs, which regularly attract about 14 per cent of old people and have undergone a rapid growth in the last decade, could provide hot and appetising mid-day meals. An experienced adviser on clubs and leisure time activities for the aged has noted that many of the existing lunch clubs, functioning once a week, produce meals of only marginal nutritional value (E. White, *Clubs for the elderly*, National Old People's Welfare Council, 1966). Secondly, if day clubs are to succeed in attracting the frail, the infirm and the isolated, then they will have to provide transport; yet a national survey found that only a fifth do so at present (G. Gibson, *New Society*, 27 August 1964).

It is impossible here to deal with other services except perhaps to pinpoint the odd example. Why, for instance, should the NHS hearing aid be more ungainly than similar devices on the private market? (P. Gregory, *Deafness and public responsibility*, Codicote Press, 1964). And why should two-fifths of a national sample of 144 grouped dwellings schemes with warden service lack a guest room? (Institute of Municipal Treasurers and Accountants, 1964).

Above all, many additional services, besides those normally available, are required if the needs of old people living in the community are to be satisfactorily met. To a large extent these should centre round the provision of adequate physical resources, especially heating facilities. A hypothermic condition is not infrequently found to be a complicating factor in deterioration in old age (L. F. Prescott, M. C. Peard, and I. R. Wallace, *British Medical Journal*, 24 November 1962), and can be effectively prevented in many cases by the provision of oil convector heaters which offer a steady increase in heat without a direct burning intensity. The provision of blankets, where these are not adequately available, would help to the same end.

Secondly, much more attention should be paid to preventing accidents in the home. Accidental falls due to lack of hand rails on the stairs, poor illumination, loose rugs on slippery surfaces, trailing electrical flexes, faulty furniture or loose slippers could be avoided by the provision of the appropriate article. Burns and scalds caused by clothing catching alight or by falls into fires should be prevented by the mandatory requirement on local authorities to provide a fireguard wherever one is missing, while the danger of accidental gas poisoning could be checked by safety devices on gas appliances and a reduction in the carbon-monoxide content of household gas.

Thirdly, the supply, where necessary, of appliances like chair commodes and wheelchairs would alleviate many problems, while the installation of manually directed shower units, which have recently been developed, would enable an old person to receive a wash who was chairbound or could not use a bath.

Fourthly, old people, particularly those who live alone or are housebound, should be provided with an effective communications system. 78 per cent of the elderly do not possess a telephone in the household in which they are living (*Financial and other circumstances of retirement pensioners*, HMSO, 1966), yet 3 per cent of old people in the community have been found to be bedfast, 11 per cent to be housebound and 22 per cent to live alone (E. Shanas, P. Townsend, *et al, op cit*, pp 23 and 263). The Hornchurch study, moreover, found that of 17 old persons living alone, only one had a telephone. The highest priority should be given to providing a telephone for every old person wishing it who either lives alone or is confined to their home.

Fifthly, a substantial diversion of financial resources towards services for the aged would enable many more of them to enjoy opportunities to which they may be regarded as entitled, but which only a small minority at present enjoy. The most obvious benefits here would be occasional outings and a regular annual holiday. One source for the large increase in holiday homes needed might be some of the present convalescent homes, now in declining use, if they could be suitably adapted and were appropriately located. But such extra monies might also be used to encourage and assist old people to move into more appropriate accommodation.

Finally, the concept of personal services must be substantially extended beyond the present restricted preoccupation with meals and housework. In particular it should also embrace such services as shopping, bathing attendance, evening relief for the family, and perhaps occasional night attendance, though if required on a regular basis it is doubtful if this could be provided reliably and on sufficient scale except within the purview of a grouped dwellings or grouped flatlets scheme. It should also include, for example, taking out crippled old people in a wheelchair, when required, since otherwise an isolated and arthritic old person may effectively be confined to the house and the local health authority's permission for granting a wheelchair may be withheld. But such an extension of the scope of the services will require a careful clarification of functions and better co-ordination than exists at present, and this is discussed in a later section.

needs unmet by local authorities

A heavy weight of evidence has now accumulated to show, not only that the national average provision of various services falls very far short of that required, but that local variations are also extremely wide. Thus the revised community care plans reveal that at the end of 1965 a substantial proportion of the 173 local authorities in England and Wales offered less than 70 per cent of the national average levels of provision in each of the main fields. These included 52 authorities who offered less than this figure for home help staffing in relation to population, 16 authorities in the case of health visitors, and 12 in the case of home nurses.

But the worst deficiencies in terms of variation occurred in the sphere of special housing. At least 103 local authorities were still offering less than 70 per cent of the national average provision per 1,000 population aged 65 and over, including 76 who were supplying less than 40 per cent of the national average and 29 who had built no sheltered housing at all. Nor on current plans are these differences likely to diminish significantly in future. It is those authorities with an already high level of provision which are launching the most ambitious targets, like the West Riding which proposes to raise the number of old people accommodated in special housing from 69.3 per 1,000 population of 65 and over in 1965 to 102.5 in 1971. Similarly, the biggest strides are being taken by those authorities with a record already well in excess of the average national performance, like Barnsley which intends an increase in its provision over the current six years from 23.9 to 118.0. A quarter of those authorities without any sheltered housing in 1965, on the other hand, will still have none at all even in 1971.

Nor is this pattern of widening inequalities confined to the area where the fastest advances are being made. Plymouth, for example, with one of the lowest home help complements in the country, is proposing to raise its ratio from 3.3 per 1,000 population aged 65 and over to only 3.4, while Oldham with one of the higher ratios at 6.6 intends to double it to 12.9.

Similarly striking variations occur too in the intensity of services as well as their extensiveness. Coatbridge in Scotland, for example, has recently been shown to offer home help services on at least five days a week to 69 per cent of its elderly households, while Preston gives the same facilities to only 3 per cent and Sheffield 7 per cent (A. Harris, *op cit*, p 20-21). Nor are these isolated instances. A meticulous examination of local variations has recently yielded the general conclusion that in services for old people " there was, if anything, a tendency for need to be negatively correlated with indices of the intensity of provision " (B. Davies, *Social needs and resources in local services*, p 195-196, Michael Joseph, 1968).

A similar impression can be gained from data available concerning services other than those detailed in the health and welfare blue book. Two important services may be mentioned here, those for the mentally infirm aged and those for the incontinent. It has been estimated in a survey in Swansea that 4.4 per cent of old people are demented, in the sense of suffering cognitive impairment rendering self-care impossible (P. L. Parsons, "Mental health of Swansea's old folk," *British Journal of Preventive Social Medicine* vol 19, p 47), while a Newcastle study has reached the comparable figure of 4.85 per cent for old people living at home with senile and arteriosclerotic dementia or other severe brain syndromes (D. W. K. Kay, P. Beamish, and M. Roth, "Old age mental disorders in Newcastle-upon-Tyne," *British Journal of Psychiatry*, vol 110, p 152). Yet a very recent survey, sponsored by the Council of the Society of Medical Officers of Health, of day centres, day hospitals, work centres, welfare homes and social clubs for these persons discovered that " few community services are specifically provided for the elderly mentally infirm and their distribution is very uneven " (G. Wigley, *Lancet*, 2 November 1968). Secondly, incontinence is known frequently to precipitate admission to a geriatric hospital and services to facilitate its management must play a crucial role in any comprehensive system of community care for the aged. A study in Sheffield found that 23 per cent of old men had occasional incontinence and 3 per cent regularly so, and for women 15 per cent and 7 per cent correspondingly (W. Hobson and J. Pemberton, *The health of the elderly at home*, 1955). Yet by 1963 only 32 per cent of areas covered by a national survey ran any laundry scheme, whether public or private (G. Gibson, *New Society*, 6 August 1964). Again it has been estimated that visiting schemes vary between contacting 1 in 5 people over 65 in Louth, Lincolnshire, to 1 in 880 in Swansea (*New Society*, 10 September 1964).

In the light of this maldistribution of services it is obviously pertinent to ask how far variations in provision are explained by variations in need. In fact recent evidence has brought to light the overriding similarity in the degree of need in different areas. An examination of the proportion of old people in 13 different areas in Britain who had difficulty in performing each of seven simple self-care functions indicated that for all except one function the proportion in a majority of the areas lay within 1 per cent of the median (A. Harris, *op cit*, table 19, p 84). Secondly, Bleddyn Davies found that his family care index, constructed as a primary measure of need, had a coefficient of variation in all local authority areas in England and Wales of less than 15. He also concluded that " most coefficients of variation of need indices are between 10 and 20, but only two co-efficients of variation of standards (of provision) indices were that small " (B. Davies, *op cit*, p 199-200). And thirdly, a study of Tyneside, confirmed by the national figures in the revised Health and Welfare plans, inferred that large variations in services for the aged do not coincide with variations in need, and that if an area is poorly provided with one service, it is unlikely that this will be compensated for by a high level of provision in some complementary or substitutable service (L. G. Moseley, " Variations in socio-medical services for the aged," *Social and economic administration*, vol 2, p 179).

How can a more even distribution of resources be ensured? It is clear that the pressure to improve below average standards of provision as a result of the publicising of local authority plans has proved inadequate. It is patently not enough for the Ministry to indulge in mealy mouthed exhortations like: "A very satisfactory feature of the plans is the number of authorities who aim to provide home helps in 1975 in excess of 1.0 per 1,000 population." (*Health and welfare, op cit*, p 13). Where standards are below certain levels, therefore, the Ministry should seek rather to establish at least minimum coverage and quality by making health and welfare grants to local authorities conditional on their upgrading services to the requisite standard within a limited period. Such grants, graded according to evidence of certain identifiable needs, are discussed below. But the point can be made here that such a system would carry the built-in possibility of a progressive improvement in standards through raising the minimum level acceptable for payment of the grant, a procedure that already satisfactorily operates for housing subsidies.

Secondly, there are at present no statutory enactments specifically *requiring* local authorities to ensure the general welfare of old people living in their own homes. In order to guarantee, therefore, that key services will be available wherever necessary, services now offered under permissive powers by local authorities should be made mandatory, whether by simple amendment of the National Assistance Act 1948 or by fresh legislation. Such services should include the provision of mobile meals, soiled laundry collection, chiropody, concessionary transport fares and sheltered workshops. Local authorities should also be empowered and encouraged to offer new services, particularly arrangements for effective heating facilities, adaptations to the home to forestall accidents, the installation, where needed, of devices to assist bathing and toileting, and the supply of a telephone to those house-bound or living alone. After a reasonable period to permit experimentation and public discussion of the most appropriate means of delivering such services, these powers also should be made mandatory.

reasons for the persistence of unmet needs

If the preceding analysis has revealed anything, it has laid bare the sheer inefficacy of consumer demand by old people. This may be explained by the widespread poverty in old age, which has been well documented, and indeed it has been recently shown that income inequalities actually widen in old age even in comparison with the disparities of working life (A. R. Prest and T. Stark, *The Manchester School of Economic and Social Studies*, vol 35, p 217). But even if financial weakness in so many subtle ways underscores the vulnerability of the aged, there can be no doubt that many other factors impair their willingness, capacity or determination to obtain the services to which they are entitled. These factors must be carefully weighed if an effective framework of community care for the elderly is to be implemented.

Firstly, conditions are often laid down for eligibility for various services which are likely, if not calculated, to deter applicants. A national survey of chiropody schemes, for example, found that only a sixth offered unqualified access: usually a doctor's certificate was required or referral by a member of the medical officer of health's department (G. Gibson, *New Society*, 13 August 1964). The home help service is sometimes only made available for short periods during time of illness, and may be refused if the old person has a daughter living in the local authority area. Most home helps are discouraged from cleaning windows, and a narrow definition of housework is often imposed which may exclude spring-cleaning (J. Tunstall, *op cit*, p 283). Again, some laundry services only accept applicants attended by a district nurse, and not all schemes collect and deliver, nor do they all loan reserve linen to their clients when their existing supplies are being laundered (G. Gibson, *New Society*, 6 August 1964). Also, charges may be imposed, sometimes involving a means test. One survey found that 8 per cent of laundry schemes charged 7s or more per collection, 5 per cent of chiropody schemes charged 5s or more per treatment (including 1 per cent which charged 9s), and 15 per cent of mobile meals schemes charged more than 1s 3d per meal (National Labour Women's Advisory Committee, *Care of the elderly*, second report, pp 17, 23 and 27, Labour Party, 1964).

Secondly, old people may be unaware of the nature or seriousness of their condition, or of services available to remedy or assist them, or both. After all, " need " is a relative concept, and an unwillingness to accept diminished powers and growing disabilities may override the prompting to seek alleviation. Also, knowledge of the social services may be very fragmentary or even non-existent. A study of 2,000 over-eighties revealed that 6 per cent did not know of any local authority or voluntary welfare service (S. Lempert, *Report on the survey of the aged in Stockport*, 1958).

Thirdly, certain conditions clearly predispose an old person to non-reporting of illness and need, particularly the isolation of the housebound and the disordered perceptions as well as the loss of social contacts engendered by mental infirmity. But it is also significant in this context to note that a sixth of chiropody schemes did not allow for domiciliary visits (G. Gibson, *op cit*).

Fourthly, a reluctance to complain or assert demands is undoubtedly a pervasive phenomenon in old age. It has been found, for example, that of old people living in households lacking all three basic facilities—sole use of fixed bath and kitchen and indoor wc—three-fifths did not acknowledge that there was anything about the dwelling which they disliked or found inconvenient (P. Townsend and D. Wedderburn, *op cit*, p 66). Furthermore, in the face of the apathy and resignation of many old people, the continued use by local authorities of grant-aided voluntary bodies to execute permissive powers to provide certain services is likely to prolong the distortion in the supply of workers and the availability of services. For this reason areas with the highest economic status (J-index) had more than six times the proportion of meals-on-wheels schemes compared to areas of lowest economic status (A. Harris, *Meals on wheels for old people*, table 73, National Council for the Care of Old People, 1960).

How can these problems of non-reporting and non-application be overcome? One requirement should be that restrictions on eligibility to schemes and artificial limitations on their scope should be removed. Charges moreover should not be imposed on any applicants falling within certain definable categories of risk, which are discussed below. But the chief question still remains as to how the whole range of needs can be much more fully elicited.

A powerful plea has been made to replace the present producer orientation of social services for old people by a consumer orientation based on market research and experiments designed to discover what old people really want (J. Tunstall, " Selling services to old people," *New Society*, 8 July 1965). A start has already been made in this direction. A Ministry of Health circular dated 10 December 1965, noting that " the size of the (home help) service is sometimes determined without full knowledge of the extent of local need for the service," suggested that authorities should undertake local studies to assess needs (Circular 15/65, paras 2 and 8). More significantly, the Ministry of Housing has inaugurated its own appraisal of self-contained flatlets at Stevenage built by its own architects who had themselves been briefed from surveys by sociologists of similar blocks of flats already built elsewhere, from user requirements in other types of accommodation, and from ergonometric studies of the physical dimensions of old people (*Design bulletin, no 11*, HMSO, 1966). The report illustrates beautifully that normal rules cannot be taken for granted with old people. Fear of intruders, for example, kept windows shut at night with consequent ventilation problems, while the amount and size of tenants' furniture was underestimated, and its actual disposition formed an ironic contrast with the neat logical clusters anticipated.

Nevertheless, it would be less than honest not to appreciate also the limitations of such an approach. A Building Research Station report, for instance, tried to discover the kind of environment old people preferred, to determine whether to construct dwellings grouped together and isolated from the homes of other age groups or integrated in blocks and estates housing young families. In fact a majority of the sample preferred to be housed among young families, as most indeed were (K. J. Haynes and J. Raven, *The living pattern of some old people*, 1966). Unfortunately for policy guidelines, however, an earlier survey by the Research Station, in which groups of old people's dwellings predominated, showed that 70 per cent of old people favoured housing in which they had old people as neighbours. This suggests that attitude surveys may only prove that old people, perhaps like other sections of the population, tend to opt for what they already have and know about, and that realistic choices can only be made on the basis of some actual experience of the alternatives. A proper consumer emphasis will therefore require a far more systematic exposition of services available to old people.

policies for prevention

A register of old people. A full consumer orientation can only be founded, however, on the precise determination of the nature, extent and location of need throughout each area. As has been frequently argued, this can only be achieved through the establishment of a comprehensive register of old people in each locality. It is therefore peculiarly unfortunate that the Seebohm Report should have concluded on this point: " we certainly do not favour any proposal to include on one list the names of all those who reach a particular age, whether they want to be on it or not; such a measure would be neither economic nor desirable " (*Report of the Committee on Local Authority and Allied Personal Social Services*, para 298, cmnd 3703, HMSO 1968). Why not, one wonders? For no reasons are given. The report goes on: " it is not for us to set out in detail for local authorities how they should identify and assess need, but we are certain that unless they can evolve a system of early detection which is suited to local circumstances, they will be unable to provide *an adequate overall service* for the old " (para 299, my emphasis). But to hope that a reasonably comprehensive coverage of needs can be achieved, whilst at the same time excluding the sole certain means to secure this end, is to adopt the tactics of the ostrich. Nor have other bodies considered that an old people's register would constitute an unwarrantable intrusion into their privacy. A report of the Royal College of Physicians of Edinburgh felt that "such an estimate of the probable attitude of old people is incorrect. In our experience the great majority of elderly people like to be visited" (*The care of the elderly in Scotland*, para 94, 1963). This judgment appears to be substantiated by a Birmingham report on the first large-scale experiment in registration. "Apart from one bellicose 90 year old gentleman, who apparently stormed the department and declared the whole thing an outrageous intrusion on his private life, there were few complaints" (*The Guardian*, 1 October 1968).

How would such a register operate, and what results can be expected? In the case of Birmingham in 1966, the Ministry of Health granted the welfare department the right to use the city's health executive council records, which offer the only virtually complete list of persons of retirement age outside the Ministry of Social Security files. The register was initially confined to the over 75 years olds, and letters were sent out inviting registration, especially of those living alone, and supplying forms on which to tick services required. The list included aids for the disabled, workshops, free bus travel, home nursing, fireguards and supplementary benefits. Some 26,380 replied, or nearly 60 per cent, including 18,960 who registered without specifying any immediate need. Of the remainder, some 45 per cent made a request for chiropody, 18 per cent for rent rebates, 15 per cent for general advice, 14 per cent for home helps, 12 per cent for free bus travel, 10 per cent for visiting, 7 per cent each for supplementary pensions, meals on wheels and health visitors, and 5 per cent for day centres (*The Times*, 10 December 1967). The validity of these requests was checked at a preliminary stage when out of 1,400 on the new register 80 per cent had asked for services, and 74 per cent were found by social workers to be in real need of the services asked for. Moreover it should be noted that these levels of hitherto unrecognised demand almost certainly represent substantial underestimates since they were based on self-assessment and old people, as has been shown, notoriously underrate their needs. Also, it may be reasonably conjectured that among the 40 per cent of non-respondents are concentrated many of those in the most desperate need since their condition often makes them the least likely to initiate a voluntary response.

Unquestionably the chief value of a comprehensive register lies not so much in the fuller ascertainment of need which it makes possible as the opportunity it presents to forge a framework of preventive services. The potential here is immense. In one preventive health clinic for the elderly in London, those examined were found to have a median of no less than eleven disabilities each, including incorrect glasses, wax in the ears, foot defects, shrinking skeleton bones and joints, diseases of the stomach and digestive system, anaemia, thyroid deficiency, heart disease, artery diseases and defective artificial teeth. The conclusion drawn from the work was that " most of these conditions, with perhaps the exception of the gross heart diseases which are unpredictable, were considerably improved under preventive treatment " (J. Maddison, *Preventing the disabilities of later life*, Middlesex, 1962). Similar inferences about the potential efficacy of preventive measures were drawn from the Edinburgh study where more than half of the existing disabilities of both men and women were unknown to the doctor.

Routine visiting and primary prevention. The countrywide implementation of old age registers, perhaps by stages, beginning with the over 75s, then those over 70 and finally all over 65, would institute the main plank in a system of primary prevention. Regular visiting and screening could then be carried out at least once a year of each person on the register at which their social and medical needs could then be carefully assessed.

The main issue arising here is who should be responsible for these visits. No single existing role within the health and welfare services automatically fits this function. General practitioners who are known already to see about 70 per cent of the old people on their lists each year (E. Shanas, P. Townsend, *et al, op cit*, p 87) have also been found to have a rather fragmentary knowledge of the social services. In one study of 52 general practitioners, only 19 had a working knowledge of five or less of eleven community services selected, though they were well aware of the hospital services chosen, and the conclusion was drawn that general practice was preoccupied with curative rather than preventive medicine (J. A. D. Anderson and E. A. Warren, *Medical officer*, vol 116, p 333). Health visitors, on the other hand, still devote only 8 per cent of their visits to old people, and the vast bulk of their work remains concerned with children under five. District nurses currently devote more than half their visits to the elderly, but the total number of cases dealt with per year has been steadily falling and is now 25 per cent below the level in 1955. Vagueness about their role is reflected in the Seebohm Committee's imprecision: " the figures *are thought* to reflect the changing pattern of work of the home nurse who now deals with cases which individually require a larger proportion of her time " (appendix F, para 247, my emphasis). But does this mean the improved intensity of service for some at the expense of the (growing) remainder in need, and does it involve the gradual substitution of para-medical services in line with lowered medical consultation rates for the elderly? Anyway, home nurses at present lack the training and skill to undertake social diagnosis. The home help service is more exclusively geared to the care of old people than any other service; 79 per cent of cases taken up in 1967 were in this field. But the service is handicapped by a dangerous over dependence on part time workers, their proportion having increased from 73 per cent in 1948 to 96 per cent in 1967 (*ibid*, para 254). Also it is clearly inappropriate to consider this service for the role of domiciliary medical assessment.

The picture therefore is of a somewhat haphazard mosaic of non-interlocking functions. Widespread efforts, however, are being made to improve co-operation. Some medical schools are laying greater stress on the role and use of the social services in the training of doctors, and the Gillie Report has urged a shift towards normal psychology and sociology in the education of the pre-clinical years (*The field work of the family doctor*, p 48, 1963). Experimental tests are being devised at Ware (Hertfordshire) to enable social workers or other non-medical personnel to carry out routine screening of old people living at home, with arrangements for the information to be analysed and passed on to general practitioners (*Sunday Times*, 28 April 1968). Indeed, if reliable tests could be constructed, it would strongly encourage a more extensive attachment of health visitors to general practice and a greater concentration of their work on the elderly now that infant mortality presents a less pressing challenge. But since health visitors still number only about a third of the total of general practitioners, such a policy would depend on a further substantial shift towards group practice since less than half of the principals at present are members of partnerships of three or more doctors. It is not enough, however, to accept locational centralisation as the panacea of co-operation. It is unhelpful to record that an adequate overall service for the old "will require co-operation and understanding at all levels in the whole community as well as a definite place known to all, to which anyone in need can be referred with the certain knowledge that appropriate action will be taken where necessary (Seebohm Report, para 299). Anatomical generalisations can provide no substitute for hard discussion of the real problems of *functional* co-ordination.

If medico-social assessment cannot be combined within a single role, then comprehensive coverage of the needs of old people in the community must be guaranteed by the establishment of a dual preventive system of routine visiting. On the medical side, it is probable that only general practitioners can undertake with full reliability the detection of incipient symptoms and the assessment of liability to ill-health. An average practice of 2,458 patients (as at 1 October 1966) is likely to include about 295 persons over 65, and since the doctor already sees some 207 (or 70 per cent) of these at least once a year, routine medical check-ups would only involve contacting an extra 88 or so old people per year. A domiciliary visit would only be necessary to those who failed to respond to an invitation to attend the surgery. Effective preventive measures would, however, entail more searching enquiries than appear sometimes at least to characterise consultations (for example, P. Townsend and D. Wedderburn, *op cit*, p 63). Of course, general practitioners would not be able to undertake exhaustive tests either, and in cases of doubt they should have the opportunity to refer patients to specialist centres, particularly chiropody, ophthalmic, otological and psychiatric clinics.

The central significance of these proposals is that psycho-geriatric assessment would shift towards a domiciliary emphasis and away from an in-patient one. The latter is now recognised to involve certain definite drawbacks: mental confusion may be prompted by the environmental change which may appear abrupt and distressing, there is a tendency in even the best hospital wards to depersonalisation, and perhaps a greater risk is created of bedsores and incontinence. Also a recent study of patients admitted to an active geriatric unit found that 72 per cent developed complications during illness in hospital, in half the cases not as a direct or indirect consequence of the condition for which they were admitted, but precipitated by their stay in hospital, and these complications were judged responsible for a seventh of the deaths (A. Rosin and R. Boyd, *Journal of Chronic Diseases,* vol 19, p 307). But even with a shift towards domiciliary examination, an in-patient psycho-geriatric assessment unit would still retain a vital role. The intricate complexity in the balance between psychiatric and physiological factors, together with the severity of the consequences of institutional misplacement, both require such a unit. For one study which found that 34 per cent of old people admitted to mental hospital were misplaced, their illness being mainly or entirely physical, while 24 per cent of those admitted to a geriatric unit were misplaced, their illness being mainly or entirely mental, also found that the mortality of misplaced patients was significantly higher and that the discharge rate of the surviving misplaced patients was significantly lower (C. B. Kidd, *British Medical Journal,* 8 December 1962). Short-term specialist assessment units under the joint care of a geriatrician and a psychiatrist would still therefore perform the essential function of securing correct institutional placement in the significant proportion of marginal cases.

In regard to social needs, probably the most effective means of developing a preventive system of social care would be, as has been often suggested, through an extension of the role of the home help. " The help needed by the elderly infirm in their own homes ranges from someone who will regularly spend a few hours doing the type of housework which necessitates kneeling or stretching, to someone who will pay daily visits and run through the gamut of duties such as would be undertaken by a solicitous relative. This will include washing, shopping, cooking, help with bodily cleanliness and simple nursing services. It may include advice on personal business matters, such as pension arrangements or payment of bills " (C. H. Wright and C. Roberts, " The place of the home help service in the care of the aged," *The Lancet,* 1 February 1958). The aim must be to substitute for the family where none exists or to supplement the resources of the family where these are inadequate or temporarily unavailable. The tasks involved may be of only brief duration, such as making beds, lighting fires, putting money in the gas meter, posting letters, or getting coal from an inaccessible coal shelter, but the accent would be on regularity.

Such a development of home help functions would also enable home nurses to concentrate on skilled nursing care, as the profession has recently been demanding (Queen's Institute of District Nursing, *Feeling the pulse,* 1967). Above all, it would impose on home helps the primary duty for systematising the haphazard methods of referral which currently operate. At present, they refer only 10 per cent of recipients of mobile meals, for example, and local authority health and welfare departments, doctors and friends or relations all refer as many or more persons (A. Harris, *Meals on wheels for old people,* table 18, National Council for the Care of Old People, 1960). Furthermore, as the main arm of a preventive service, the home help would be the member of the new social service department envisaged by the Seebohm Committee who would visit both those old people who failed to reply to the annual letter asking if any social services were required and those who requested a visit so that general advice about services could be personally given. Nor should the former responsibility constitute a very onerous addition to other duties. Since there were 29,008 whole time equivalent home helps at 30 September 1967, there exists a mean per home help of approximately 230 persons aged 65 and over in Britain (bearing in mind that only 79 per cent of the case load of home helps embraces the care of old people), and if on the Birmingham experience 60 per cent reply to the annual circular it would entail about an extra 92 visits a year. Again, meeting the demand for a family advisory service might involve, on the Birmingham model, a mean of perhaps 20 further visits per year for each home help.

What would be the implications of these proposals for the recruitment, training and deployment of home helps? Firstly and most obviously, they would require a faster growth in the staffing of the service than has so far been intended, even though an improvement in the whole time equivalent ratio to a mean of one per 154 persons over 65 (again assuming the devotion of four-fifths of the caseload to the needs of old age) is anticipated by 1975 in the latest revision of the ten year plans. A rise in the recruitment of the scale required can only be produced by making the job much more attractive, and increased responsibilities must be reflected in increased pay.

Secondly, the creation of an effective system of referral will demand training to produce an accurate working knowledge of the functioning of the social services, and the professional standards derived from the training should act as a further inducement to the job. Certainly, better pay and training ought to move the employment pattern away from its over-dependence on part time workers and offer a service less marked by irregular periods between visits. For the present rate of turnover must be substantially reduced and the distribution of employment, whereby

55 per cent of the visits are on a twice weekly basis for two or three hours per time, must be altered.

Risk registers. Within a comprehensive system of routine visiting and medico-social assessment, the next step in the development of a fully preventive service should be to define special categories of risk in order to crystallise limited resources of personnel and time on the early detection of deterioration and to improve the chances of remedial action. Therefore, the main risk groups might well be classified as follows:

1. The severely incapacitated. These can be defined as those scoring 7 points or more on a 0-12 points scale embracing personal care, sensory abilities and the capacity to perform certain physical tasks necessary to maintain an independent household (P. Townsend, "Measuring incapacity for self care," in Williams, Tibbitts and Donahue, *Processes of ageing,* vol 2, p 272, Atherton Press, 1963).

2. The mentally infirm, defined either by the Tooting Bec scale of cognitive impairment (J. W. L. Doust, *et al, Journal of Mental Diseases,* vol 117, p 397-8) or a social maladaption scale including as items verbal confusion, physical restlessness or wandering, disorientation of person or situation, disorientation of place, and anormic behaviour (M. Meacher, *Taken for a ride*: special residential homes for confused old people: a study of segregation in social policy, forthcoming).

3. Those subject to extreme social isolation. The phenomenon of extreme isolation can be rated on the basis of less than 5 social contacts within the previous week. (J. Tunstall, *Old and alone,* p 82, Routledge, 1966).

4. The extreme aged, taken as those aged over 85.

The selection of these four groups has been necessarily rather arbitrary, but there is reason to believe that they include a very high proportion of the most vulnerable section among the elderly. Research has begun to expose the close association between these factors and other known susceptible states of old age. The authors of one study, for example, claim to have detected a senile breakdown syndrome which they discovered chiefly among women over 70 of independent and domineering personality who become subject to isolation, bereavement or alcoholism (D. Macmillan and P. Shaw, *British Medical Journal,* 29 October 1966). J. Tunstall has illustrated the strong connection between loneliness and widowhood and physical incapacity, and has also shown that extreme isolation is more common in rural areas so that its inclusion here would draw attention to the special unmet needs of old people in the country (H. C. Miller, *The ageing countryman,* National Council for the Care of Old People, 1963). Social isolation is also known to be strongly

ESTIMATED NUMBERS OF OLD PEOPLE IN HIGH-RISK GROUPS IN BRITAIN, 1964

risk classification	number aged 65 and over
severe incapacity	350,000
mental infirmity	277,000
extreme social isolation	262,000
age over 85	305,000

associated with suicide and depression in old age (E. Stengel, " The causation and prevention of suicide in old age," in *Psychiatric Disorders in the Aged,* p 56, 1965). Furthermore, the acute vulnerability of patients discharged from geriatric hospitals is known to be connected with extreme age and physical frailty (J. C. Brocklehurst and M. Shergold, *The Lancet,* 23 November 1968).

The other factors which determined the selection of these four categories were precision and manageability. Whatever at-risk classification is adopted, it should enable the concentration of resources to be accurately directed to a comparatively few points of greatest need. Thus the construction of a risk register for infants (M. Sheridan, *Monthly Bulletin of the Ministry of Health,* vol 21, p 238) has been criticised on the grounds that a strict application of the criteria would mean including 60-70 per cent of all new-born babies (T. E. Oppé, *Developmental Medicine and Child Neurology,* vol 9, p 13). The groups in the proposed at-risk register for old age, however, the numbers of which are given in the table above would not embrace more than 20 per cent of all old people even if the various categories were mutually exclusive, which they certainly are not. Secondly the definitions should be manageable in the sense that they can be readily applied by simple tests in the field, and the scales referred to above could no doubt be refined for this purpose. It can of course be argued that a sharp focusing on certain minorities is in danger of causing others to be neglected who may equally be afflicted by a number of disabilities. But this is a hazard which is surely outweighed by the utility of locating at least a large majority of the most vulnerable persons, and anyway annual routine screening should remain effective with the remainder.

How should the information be compiled and used? Perhaps the most suitable vehicle for the collection of this data would be the research and intelligence unit which the Seebohm Committee recommends be set up in each major local authority area (para 466). When collected, the information should be made available to both general practitioners and the home help organiser in the social service department, and it should be made the basis of a more intensive system of routine checks, perhaps involving at least quarterly contact. Even this degree of systematisation, however, would of course still fail in many cases if it is not combined with better co-ordination between hospital and local authority services. One method of improving liaison which has recently received favourable comment from a number of sources is the attachment to a geriatric unit of a district nurse or health visitor who acts as a bridge by reporting social difficulties to the social service department and medical ones to the patient's general practitioner (for example, N. H. Nisbet, *et al, The Lancet,* 11 June 1966). But vital though it is, this problem lies outside the immediate scope of this essay.

Secondary prevention. The discussion so far has been limited to the question of detecting and remedying incipient breakdown. At an earlier point social policy could perhaps enable even this liability to be forestalled to some extent by enabling roles to be preserved into old age so far as possible. For several studies have shown that " non-senile " personality patterns are associated with active social roles, especially within the family, the retention of group and individual relationships, interest in a variety of activities, interest in the future and continued work (R. Albrecht, " Social roles in the prevention of senility," *Gerontology Journal,* vol 5, p 386). This goal could therefore be pursued in at least two directions: the protection of the extended family structure with its internal distribution of functions and the extension of employment opportunities beyond the normal retirement age.

Now so far from strengthening extended family ties, it is well known that certain processes of social policy directly undermine them. Rehousing programmes have in the past ignored the effect on the family network and the ensuing isolation of the eldest generation (M. Young and P. Wilmott, *Family and kinship in East London,* 1957). Even now old people who say they want to be near their children as their reason for desiring to move are not assisted by housing authorities " no Authority gives this as one of the factors taken into account when deciding the need for rehousing " (A. Harris, *Social welfare for the elderly,* vol 1, p 37-38, HMSO, 1968).

In contrast to such short-sightedness, imaginative policies are needed to integrate old people into the fabric of family life wherever they have lost or been separated from their own families. One scheme adopted by the American War on Poverty Programme in this connection has been to link old people with retarded children as foster grandparents (N. Fendell, Paper to the World Mental Health Conference, 1968). Another scheme which has been tried in a number of towns in this country has been the boarding out of old people with families in the district, and the National Council of Social Service has found that " many of the elderly people who are not able to live quite alone, or have no settled home, soon adapt themselves well with a family " (*New Society,* 12 September 1963).

Against this it is often declared that old people, especially if they become physically or mentally infirm, impose an unreasonable burden on their family. But the evidence does not substantiate this view. A survey of 1,115 old people discharged from a geriatric unit judged that only 12 (or 1.2 per cent) relatives unreasonably refused to provide home care, and that a willingness to accept the care of severely disabled patients was five times more common (C. P. Lowther and J. Williamson, " Old people and their relatives," *The Lancet*, 31 December 1966). A national study examining the role of the family in illness and infirmity found that for old people needing help in personal care or household chores, half received such help from the spouse, child or other relative at home, a tenth or more from a child, relative or friend outside the household, and only some 7 per cent from the social services (P. Townsend and D. Wedderburn, *op cit*, tables 11-15). A detailed evaluation of the effects of caring for the aged at home concluded that " there is no doubt that many families prefer to have their sick patient at home, even if this does impose hardship . . . In visiting homes, especially those of elderly couples where one partner had become ill, we were most impressed by the amount of hardship people will gladly endure to avoid their patient being admitted. This appears not just a fear of stigma, but of loneliness and a wish to care for their patient themselves " (J. Grad and P. Sainsbury, *British Journal of Psychiatry*, vol 114, p 265).

Community care does not seem less effective. The last study referred to in the previous paragraph also found that though in Salisbury hospital admissions were made at double the rate of Chichester, the outcome of the patients' illnesses after two years did not materially vary. Significant differences in the impact on the families concerned were registered only in terms of the relief of the *less* serious or *less* socially conspicuous consequences of the disorder, like contrariness in the old person or the need to provide constant companionship. With regard to the more serious symptoms, like loss of employment or ill-health of family members caused by the patient or dangerous or objectionable behaviour of the patient, the hospital-based service offered no greater relief than the community-based one, despite the fact that in the latter " the social services and domiciliary nursing are very sketchy."

We may therefore conclude that so far from giving an impression of an intolerable burden, the evidence suggests that not only does maintaining an old person within the circle of constant family interaction offer a powerful preventive therapy, but such a policy is also positively supported by a very large majority of families themselves.

The second central aim of social planning in terms of secondary prevention should be the deliberate extension of occupational opportunity beyond the normal age of retirement. The research literature offers an abundant weight of evidence that abrupt and enforced retirement is much resented and that for working-class men in particular it can constitute a disastrous loss of function for the remaining years of life. Moreover for all age groups over 65 Britain's employment rate is considerably lower than those in Denmark and the United States, for example (E. Shanas, P. Townsend, *et al, op cit*, p 294, table 7).

What is particularly missed in retirement? For 507 workers interviewed at Slough " paid employment was to them more than the money involved; it gave them status and made them feel part of the community " (*Workers nearing retirement*, Nuffield Foundation, 1963). Whilst in the cross-national study only 4 per cent of retired men over 65 declared they missed most the work itself and 24 per cent the money, 10 per cent mentioned the people at work and 5 per cent a sense of feeling useful (E. Shanas, P. Townsend *et al, op cit*, p 334, table 8). This suggests that perhaps a fifth would welcome a return to employment or some manageable part time activity or at least some occupational diversion if confined by infirmity within their homes. Indeed 29 per cent of retired men over 65 without incapacity and 11 per cent with moderate incapacity expressed a desire for work (*ibid*, p 389, table 11). Also it has been found that of men over 65 staying at work, 55 per cent did so for non-economic reasons, either because they felt fit enough or they preferred to work (Ministry of Pensions and National Insurance, *Reasons given for retiring or continuing at work*, HMSO, 1954).

What type of employment then could those over 65 — particularly men, but increasingly also women now that they form a third of the labour force — satisfactorily undertake? Some observers have tended to be pessimistic. One has concluded that older manual workers, despite greater patience, exactitude and craftsmanship, cannot compensate on the conveyor belt for their failing physical powers and slower reactions. Yet at the same time most of the " light " jobs traditionally reserved for old people tend to be suitable for mechanisation, while those which remain tend to be reserved for the young disabled worker (F. Le Gros Clark, *Work, age and leisure*, Michael Joseph, 1966). This confirms the Medical Research Council survey of ageing and the semi-skilled on Merseyside which found that the range of alternative work considered suitable for older men is often narrowly restricted to cleaning, sweeping and other menial tasks.

Other investigators, however, believe that the unrealised potential of older workers is considerable, given certain appropriate conditions. Psychologists have shown that in vocabulary, information and reading capacity, ability steadily *grows* with age, provided the elderly person has not lost interest or failed to practise (J. Latimer, *Journal of Genetics and Psychology*, vol 102). Tests have shown that older persons can learn almost anything to the same degree of proficiency as younger people, provided they are given sufficient time to learn it, are taught by demonstration and practical application rather than by detailed verbal instruction, and are not embarrassed by invidious comparisons in the presence of younger persons. A. T. Welford concludes in a classic study that though problem-solving capacities gradually decline, there is increasing variability between one person and another as the age scale is ascended, and that even where age changes do impinge on performance, a relatively slight change in the task can often bring it well within the capacities of older people (A. T. Welford, *Ageing and human skill*, OUP, 1958).

Present employment practices, however, scarcely reflect the social benefit which could be derived from preserving occupational involvement into old age. The economic activity tables in the 1966 sample census reveal that most manual jobs, which are often those chiefly affected by compulsory retirement rules together with a high degree of ill-health and considerable physical strain, contain well below the national average of 3.6 per cent male workers over 65. Those jobs with the largest proportion of older workers appear to be in the clothing and footwear trades, the distributive trades, professional and scientific services, and various other service occupations.

A much more determined effort should therefore be made to find suitable employment in old age, particularly for semi-skilled and unskilled manual workers who may find it harder to develop alternative satisfying interests after retirement. A few firms have experimented with a part time department for retired workers where individual assembly work is undertaken for a limited number of hours each morning, and since a man is paid by the hours worked, he can stay at home if he feels unwell or overtired. But the implementation of such schemes is still haphazard, and the *social* benefits of this and alternative experiments have not been carefully evaluated. Also, the process of obtaining jobs in old age needs a radical overhaul. Of a sample of 504 retired but re-employed men and women in Luton, only 1 per cent found their new job through the Employment Exchange, though 40 per cent had made application to this source. In fact, 52 per cent found their jobs through voluntary agencies, 23 per cent by means of advertisements, and a further 23 per cent through a personal approach (D. R. Snellgrove, *Elderly employed*, White Crescent Press, 1963). Various Councils of Social Service have set up employment bureaux for retired men in a number of cities, but a comprehensive rationale in the distribution of jobs can only be fully achieved by broadening the responsibilities of the existing national network of employment exchanges to include the special duty to study the capacities of older workers and to seek out a pattern of job opportunities appropriate for this specific group. Wherever possible, employment should be sought on the open market, and the Government should give serious thought to a subsidy policy for private firms designed to secure the widest possible acceptance of older workers in industry. But where ill-health or incapacity renders such job attainment difficult or impossible, the role of sheltered workshops must be more systematically explored. Trade unions on their part should negotiate special rates of pay for older workers, as they have done for the disabled. Lastly, these policies must also entail the relaxation, if not the outright abolition, of the earnings rule which at present usually enforces a choice between full time work or acceptance of the pension without work, since part time work at the appropriate wage is not easy to find.

the cost of community care

Realistic politics will demand that an extension of community care on the scale envisaged must involve a reallocation of expenditure between domiciliary and residential services. Indeed a shift of emphasis is certainly called for as in 1967-68 some £43.8 millions was devoted to residential homes for the aged and infirm, containing 106,840 persons, while the three central domiciliary services for old people—home helps, district nursing and health visiting—consumed only £41.1 millions, of which perhaps £25 millions was expended on the care of the elderly (*Annual report of the Ministry of Health for* 1967, tables 51, 57 and 58, cmnd 3702, HMSO, 1968). Since these three community services embrace some 1,153,000 old people, perhaps half as much again is spent on residential welfare as on the main domiciliary services, though the latter reach more than ten times the number of persons assisted by the former.

The argument for a large and planned shift of resources towards community care is buttressed by the limited economic data available on comparative costs. One tentative analysis, undertaken in a part of Lancashire containing 24,000 old people, found that in only about 1 per cent of cases of those receiving domiciliary care did the cost exceed that of maintenance in a welfare home, and that in only a further 1 per cent did the cost of community services reach four-fifths of the cost of residential care. Furthermore, in less than 0.1 per cent of cases did the cost of domiciliary care equal that of the cheapest hospital bed (J. Dixon, *Domiciliary costs survey,* unpublished, 1957-58). A similar conclusion was reached in an inquiry at a day hospital in Durham which claimed that the day care offered could meet the medical and physiotherapeutic needs of many old people at less than a quarter of the cost of in-patient care in similar cases (*The Almoner,* October 1964). Also the plea for a sizeable increase of investment in sheltered housing can be made at least as much on economic as on social grounds when the capital cost of such units is only about £1,500, compared with about £1,900 for a place in a residential home (D. Paige and K. Jones, *Health and welfare services in* 1975, p 97, CUP, 1966).

For once therefore social and economic pressures mutually reinforce each other in urging a shift of emphasis towards domiciliary care. In implementing such a change of balance, the Government should take the opportunity to extend those techniques of positive discrimination which already characterise its policy towards educational priority areas, the urban programme and the recently announced community development project. It has already been suggested that by replacing the block grant with a series of specific health and welfare grants, the Government could establish minimum domiciliary staffing ratios by making such grants dependent on the achievement of at least minimum standards, which could then be progressively raised. But in addition a more equitable distribution of resources could be secured by scaling these grants according to the proportion in each local authority area of old people within the four main risk-groups as delineated here. The data to be used in grading the payments would be derived from the returns made by local authorities based on the researches of their intelligence units as proposed by the Seebohm Report. Thus the areas with the highest proportions of old people in the most vulnerable categories should be able to provide services commensurate with the greater degree of local need. Perhaps then we will have established at least the basic structure of preventive services for old people in this country comparable to those for children, originally enunciated by section 48 of the Ingleby Report and given legislative substance by section 1 of the Childrens and Young Persons Act, 1963.

summary of proposals

1. The Government should declare an unequivocal commitment to reverse the emphasis of social policy in old age from care in institutions to care in the wider community. This should be based not only on considerations of cost-effectiveness or on the well-documented pathologies of institutional life, but on the urgent need to give priority to developing preventive services and to keeping the individual within the therapeutic framework of the family circle and the surrounding network of friends and neighbours, with its interchange of services between generations.

2. On the grounds of the enormous discrepancy between the extent of needs confirmed by repeated surveys and the national level of provision, even as intended in future according to the revised community care plans, the change of emphasis in policy should be reflected in a disproportionate allocation of resources within the health and welfare budget to domiciliary services for the old.

3. Since the extent and quality of provision varies very greatly between local authorities, and not in a manner correlated with variations in local needs, central policy should be directed towards achieving a more even distribution of services. First, the block grant should be replaced by specific health and welfare grants, which should be conditional on the achievement of at least minimum standards of provision. Such a minimum could then be systematically raised over a period of time. Secondly, the permissive powers whereby such services for old people as mobile meals, laundry, chiropody, concessionary fares and workshops lie at present within the discretion of local authorities, should be made mandatory.

4. In addition, greater vigilance is required from local authorities in detecting needs

which fall outside the purview of existing provision. Where necessary, imaginative new services should be introduced. These should include ensuring that adequate heating is available in the home, that preventable accidents are obviated by the provision of the appropriate household articles, that more appliances are furnished to assist the care of the physically handicapped at home, that telephones are offered to the housebound and those who live alone, that holidays are made much more widely available, that the concept of personal services is greatly extended. The aim is not to thrust unwanted services on to indifferent recipients, but consciously to seek to raise the welfare expectations of old people as the standards of the wider community gradually rise.

5. Part of the reason why such an enormity of unmet needs persists in old age is that certain unreasonable restrictions have been imposed both in determining eligibility to various services and in framing their scope. Such restrictions, including means tests, should be removed and services should be provided free to those within definable categories of risk.

6. The major reason for under use even of existing provision remains the psychology of old people which renders the traditional procedure of self-application inadequate as a means of ensuring full take-up of required services. A comprehensive register of old people should therefore be drawn up as the sole means of determining precisely the nature, extent and location of need throughout each area, and the Ministry of Social Security should give access to its records for this purpose. Only in this way can a universal framework of preventive health and welfare services for the aged be effectively organised.

7. The Seebohm recommendation of a unified Social Service Department may improve the referral system for such services as mobile meals and home helps by combining them under a single authority, but the report equivocates on which particular role should be delegated with the chief responsibility for co-ordinating care for the aged. At present, no role within the health and welfare services is uniquely qualified for the task of assessing both health and welfare needs in old age. The function of routine annual visiting and screening should therefore be divided between the general practitioner for the assessment of medical needs and a new kind of home help for the appraisal of social needs.

8. These proposals would mean that psycho-geriatric assessment would shift towards a domiciliary emphasis and away from an in-patient one. For the latter is now recognised to involve definite drawbacks. However, for more exhaustive tests in cases of doubt, general practitioners should have the opportunity to refer patients to specialist centres, and short-term in-patient assessment units should still try to prevent institutional misplacement with its devastating consequences.

9. To fulfil the role outlined here, the concept of home help service must not only be expanded to embrace the whole range of duties from those normally performed by a solicitous relative to assistance with problems of a business nature, but above all must include the knowledge and training to systematise the present haphazard framework of referrals for social services. The large increase in the numbers and qualifications of the home helps required can only be brought about by improved pay dependent on the professional standards derived from training.

10. Within this general system of screening, special categories of risk should be defined for particular attention. These categories should be drawn narrowly enough to take in no more than perhaps 20 per cent of old people and might therefore include the severely incapacitated, the mentally infirm, the extremely isolated and the extreme aged, since these conditions are closely associated with other known vulnerable states in old age. Responsibility for identifying these groups in each locality should lie with the research and intelligence units which Seebohm proposes for each major local authority area. Once identified, these persons should be visited at 3-monthly intervals in order that preventive measures can be effectively applied on behalf of those most exposed to ill-health or social need. Furthermore, to ensure a more even distribution of resources, the specific health and welfare grants already advocated should be scaled according to the proportion of old people in each area who fall into these four categories.

11. A co-ordinated programme of longitudinal research studies, sponsored jointly by the Government, the Social Science Research Council and the social welfare and medical foundations, should be directed towards systematising data on the social and medical antecedents of breakdown in old age so that preventive policies can be brought into operation at ever earlier stages.

12. In addition to these policies of primary prevention, measures of secondary prevention should be implemented to forestall liability to breakdown through enabling the preservation of significant social roles into retirement. Such measures should chiefly involve keeping the family together and extending employment opportunities in old age.

13. Since re-housing programmes can severely undermine the flow of relationships and exchange of services within the extended family structure, one essential criterion in re-housing policy should be to preserve the daily unity of the inter-generational family. Where it has been broken, local authorities should give high priority to re-unification by re-housing isolated old persons near their families where they wish it. Such a policy is supported by many research findings that the great majority of families would prefer to have an elderly member living with or near them even if such an arrangement does involve some significant element of extra burden. On

these grounds more attention should also be paid by local authorities to experiments with boarding out old people who have lost contact with their families.

14. Since repeated surveys have shown that a sizeable proportion of men subjected to enforcement retirement would like to return to some form of work, the social benefits as a preventive measure, as well as the economic possibilities, of making more work widely available after the normal retirement age should be much more carefully evaluated. The Department of Employment and Productivity should instruct employment exchanges to seek out a pattern of job opportunities in each locality appropriate for this particular age group. Also the Government should seriously examine a subsidy policy for private firms designed to secure a much more general acceptance of older workers in industry.

7. the old: hospital and community care

John Agate

In the past twenty years there has been built up a remarkable geriatric service in the United Kingdom. It owes its origins, first, to a small group of pioneer doctors who began a new specialty, seeing a totally neglected field; secondly, the coming of the National Health Service, which provided a more equitable distribution of funds for running and eventually improving hospitals for the elderly and for paying the necessary numbers of nurses, doctors and other workers to staff them; thirdly, to a legacy of many old workhouses mostly founded under the Poor Law. These latter, though when taken over in 1948 were found to be deplorably equipped and utterly cheerless, nevertheless gave the new idea a place from which to start. Great strides have been made in the twenty years, though this hopeful generalisation may be more applicable to general hospital than to mental hospital provision for older people. Now there are more than 250 geriatric physicians, mostly experienced consultants giving full time service to the National Health Service and concentrating exclusively on the actual problems of old age. These doctors are running broadly-based area services providing for the total care of elderly people who are too ill (for the time being) to be looked after in their varying home circumstances. There are still some backward areas and still some sub-standard old hospitals but generally these are striving to reach a uniform high standard of accommodation and care.

Geriatrics is in process of rising from being the Cinderella of hospital activities, short of everything including interested professional workers, to become a potent therapeutic and health-educational force. British Geriatric Medicine is in fact the envy of many other countries; yet in the United Kingdom it is still not fully appreci-ated for what it has achieved. Its pioneers were often directly encouraged by local opinion, which had been made anxious by the size of the many problems to be solved.

the results of geriatric hospital work

In the days before 1948 the so-called " chronic sick " wards and hospitals in Britain had nurses who gave devoted services in unbelievably bad working conditions; but they were far too few in number, they had no special training, and they had minimal medical support. Treatment was negligible, comfort non-existent, and the results bad. A patient once admitted had usually to stay in bed and did not leave the place till death released him—often without the benefit of an accurate diagnosis. The " turnover " was accordingly low, waiting lists were long, and dissatisfaction was rife. In the diminishing number of areas where geriatric hospitals are not well organised this may, regrettably, still be true. However, pursuing active policies the modern geriatric physician can achieve a high " turnover " and reduce his waiting list to a nominal level except at the time of peak demand in late winter. In an area so served, ill old people can quickly get the treatment they need. The way has been shown. If the service is not up to standard in certain localities, then local demand must be voiced in order to get established a properly based geriatric department under a consultant with special knowledge and interest. Once such a doctor is appointed results will surely follow.

In broad terms a good hospital geriatric department pursuing a liberal admission policy (that is, *not* rejecting the dying, or those it believes it cannot cure) ought, notwithstanding, to be able to send back about sixty per cent of the patients it admits improved and fit to live in the community once more. True, some of them will not be fully fit; some will have residual disabilities not calling for regular medical and nursing care; many will need domestic aid of some kind. But if they do not leave hospital when they should, there will be no room for those falling ill and coming on behind. *So, modern geriatrics can now rehabilitate more older people than the social services can reintegrate into society.* This is the challenge of geriatrics to the local authority services as at present constituted. The old notion that once he enters a hospital an old person will be there for the rest of his life is quite outdated. Sometimes events turn out this way, but strenuous efforts are made to try to prevent it; yet when therapeutics and rehabilitation fails, hospital care is not begrudged to the longer-term patient and the dying. Continuing care in these circumstances is one of the duties a geriatric department willingly accepts—and other hospital departments generally speaking do not!

relations between hospital and community care

Hospital and community care are, of course, interdependent. All departments of a hospital must first maintain direct links with the family and friends of the invalid, and none needs to do so more than the geriatric department. The hospital requires its own social workers to maintain the link. They must be available day by day for interviews and consultations. Yet often, either because friends and relatives are lacking, or reluctant (or occasionally even hostile), links with the outside world have to be maintained with the help of the welfare department also. In cases of complete breakdown, where even domiciliary supporting services could not maintain the patient independently at home, then the hospital depends on the welfare department to provide residential care.

Frequently it is suggested that there are old people needing hospital treatment waiting in bed in welfare department homes and vice versa. This still happens sometimes when relations are bad and resources on both sides are strained, though it is highly unsatisfactory that it should happen. But if the hospital geriatric department has set its own house in order and reduced its waiting list to nothing, and is ready to admit upon demand, can the same be said of the welfare department? Unfortunately, in most cases it cannot. Welfare departments' waiting lists of people seeking residential places are in general rising, outstripping even their new capital programmes. Meanwhile many active geriatric departments have ten per cent or more of their places occupied by people fit to be in residential homes but waiting indefinitely for this sort of accommodation. This hampers hospital work, whilst the per capita cost is much higher in hospital than in a home. Relations between thedepartments at officer level are usually cordial, but long term limitations of resources and especially of loan sanction for the building of new homes results in a stalemate. In the face of such frustration the question then to be asked is—whether local authority policy as to the current use of residential homes for the elderly and the need to build more and more of them, is correct? Perhaps there are other solutions, such as the provision of much more sheltered housing (*Report of the Committee on local authority and allied personal social services,* Seebohm Report, paras 421-423, cmnd 3703, HMSO, 1968).

Furthermore, in most places there are quite insufficient numbers of home helps, meals-on-wheels facilities, health visitors, and even home nurses, to satisfy the domiciliary requirements of older people fit enough to leave hospital, but not yet, and perhaps never to be, completely independent. It is important to recognise that, far from being discharged against their own inclination and the wishes of everybody concerned, many elderly patients actively *desire* to leave hospital as soon as they can. The props they need exist but they are very variable in distribution and effectiveness, as might be expected where their provision is a permissive rather than an obligatory function of local authority departments, themselves split up. In country districts the difficulties seem to be multiplied, and poor housing in remote places is a particularly serious deterrent to getting an elderly patient home.

An additional problem for the hospital service is the number of channels which have to be used to obtain domiciliary and other services. For home helps one has to apply to one officer, for a home nurse perhaps to another; for home nursing equipment to a voluntary organisation supported indirectly by a local authority grant; for a personal wheelchair for a patient to a ministry depot miles away, and for an adaptation to a house to allow a person to live at home in spite of residual disability, to the Housing Manager. There is no common channel of outward communication, yet in any individual case the local authority can have a single inwards channel: at home the welfare department can get medical advice by approaching the patient's own doctor, who can call in a second opinion if need be: when needing information about a patient already in hospital the welfare department can approach the consultant direct, or at one remove go to his geriatric medical social worker if that is preferred. In practice there may be weeks of delay in getting a hospital patient resettled, and the worse delay is often in getting the minor adaptation like a ramp or an extra bannister fixed to help an old person who has had a mild stroke.

In one typical recent example an elderly patient with obesity and hip disease had been successfully rehabilitated in hospital, having shown great courage in adversity. All she needed to make life at home possible (and this was what she desired more than anything) was a ramp to help her over an awkward step from her kitchen to scullery. The hospital, asking the local authority for this provision, sent a drawing with full measurements. The materials might have cost 30s, the labour £2 at most. Four weeks later the hospital's letter was acknowledged. Some time later the Authority sent an official to check the measurements, and then proceeded to put the job out to tender. Eventually the ramp was provided, about 14 weeks after the the original request was made. Meanwhile the cost to the National Health Service of unnecessarily keeping the patient in hospital was about £235. Then, within 36 hours of the patient's return home the local authority's officials, finding they could not provide the domestic help needed, persuaded the patient to give up her home and enter a welfare home!

The hospital, often acting hopefully, may be driven by such frustration to start domestic resettlement manoeuvres as soon as the patient enters its wards, when really the full extent of the need is not yet clear. Certainly, geriatric hospitals could have a higher turnover and therefore give a better, cheaper service if it were not for these frustrations. It must be said that geriatric physicians seem to have been best served in the sphere of domiciliary aftercare when the appropriate services are all in the direct control of a co-operative Medical Officer of Health, and best of all if the Medical Officer of Health also exercises the functions of the Chief Welfare Officer. But how few do.

medical content of the problems of old age

The fact that disease in old age is often remediable in whole or in part has already been referred to. Elderly men and women must not expect to enter hospital and renounce the world at that point; nor must their families be led to expect this.

But the opinion seems to be held in some circles that the basic problem of old age is a social one and not medical. It is held that if only social conditions—housing, feeding, companionship and domestic support—were regulated properly, there would be little morbidity and no real " problem " at all. Attractive though this theory is, it is not true in fact. Times without number physicians see old people in very poor conditions yet managing fairly well and presenting no particular problem to their friends and the officials; it is not until some major disease strikes that any grave problem appears. The resilience of some old people is truly remarkable. It may be argued that the social conditions must have precipitated the disease which caused the breakdown. Sometimes this is true: but in geriatric work we are also dealing with long-term disorders with which people now arrive as they come to old age; again, there is a vast territory of degenerative disease (including heart and

H

stroke illnesses); there is malignancy; there are endocrine disorders; there are long term or recurrent old age psychiatric disorders, and it would be quite unrealistic if there were all attributed simply to adverse social conditions. Elsewhere I have previously drawn attention to a series of disorders of older people which can usefully be classified together as "Diseases of deprivation"—that is, deprivation of food and vitamins, fluids, heat, affection and incentives (J. N. Agate, "Diseases of deprivation" *Proceedings of Royal Society of Medicine,* vol 61, p 919-922). This group, together with accidents, constitutes the current preventive field for geriatrics. But as a group these disorders only make up a proportion of the geriatric hospitals' burden, and the aetiology in many such cases is a question of multiple factors, and these may be difficult to dientangle. If these preventable disorders were fully recognised, if detection was early, if housing, feeding and so on were all made satisfactory, and health education reached the old people concerned, there would still be cases of domestic accidents and deprivation, and the sum total of hospital illness in old age would perhaps be reduced, but only by a little. The plain fact is that morbidity rises almost logarithmically with age after childhood. At 85 there is a 65 per cent chance of not being fully fit, and a 10 per cent chance of already being a permanent invalid. Besides, many old people of this very great age or even less than this age, will need considerable personal aid, and are at best so-called " frail ambulant " persons. This will apply wherever they may be. *So provision for the needs of older people must have full regard to medical facts.* These facts are not properly understood even by the majority of doctors, since geriatrics is (with a few exceptions) largely ignored in the medical schools. Geriatric physicians have learnt by practical experience and cannot but be aware that the medical and social facets of their patients' cases are closely interlinked. They must regard with grave disquiet any proposal for a social service system where all the arrangements to be made locally for the care of older people outside hospital, and the necessary decisions about the fate of individuals, were to be the responsibility of social workers acting without expert medical opinion.

hospitals and homes as providers of "institutional" care

Geriatric hospital departments on the British pattern, if run on active and liberal lines, can and do usually provide the service needed, but they can only do so if they have enough resources, beds and staff for the job to be done. In many cases they provide a high standard of care and comfort at much less cost per week than that of keeping a patient in an expensive " acute ward " of a large general hospital. What is required of them is ready advice to the family doctor, rapid admission when the need arises, a real welcome for the patient whatever the nature of his malady, accurate diagnosis, prompt treatment, rehabilitation and resettlement. The geriatric hospital must also provide longer-term care or nursing in terminal illness if these are impracticable at home. Many departments also organise intermittent care or

" holiday " care in the summer. Obviously the older patient must have the right, relative to the immediate needs of others, to hospital care without a struggle if the indications are clear; but here the decisions are primarily medical ones, even if social factors loom large. Obviously too, it must be wrong to admit as a hospital in-patient anyone whose problems are entirely social. The distinction is quite easy to draw with experience in the field. Conversely it is essential also to take the view that no patient should occupy a hospital bed when his need for it has passed. Yet geriatric departments are always beset with discharge difficulties and have no power to enforce discharge whence the patient came, even if conditions are known to be suitable and promises have been made by those concerned. In the interests of keeping the hospital service viable it is tempting to ask for legislation to enforce the patient's discharge in cases of clear-cut obligation. But presumably no government would face the implications of this.

The role of welfare homes in providing " institutional " care seems now less certain than it was, in spite of their recent rapid proliferation. Until quite recently welfare authorities believed that once installed in a home an old person had an inalienable right to his place *sine die*—as long as he remained reasonably fit. Now there is more talk of people entering homes temporarily for the relief of domestic stress, as the Seebohm Report also envisages (para 304). This is clearly good sense from all points of view, but a significant proportion of the present day residents are likely to have to be " permanent " on grounds of having no suitable home, or of social incompetence, or frailty, or residual yet " manageable " physical or mental disability. However there is much to be said for strictly limiting admission into residence to the people in precisely these categories, and *not* permitting anyone to take up permanent residence who is capable of living alone or in sheltered housing. At present the general impression so often gained in the more high grade and better furnished homes is that the residents have been selected for " acceptability " and personal independence, while the less favourably endowed individuals have difficulty in getting placed. Much of this seeming " discrimination " may be determined by staffing shortages and by confusion as to the role which residential homes ought to be playing. In other words some form of significant social or other disability *not* amounting to a hospital-care problem should perhaps be the basic criterion for admission. This presupposes a proper supply of good special and protected housing for the remainder and of this there is a very great lack at present. As to location, it is clear that protected housing, grouped round a residential home which can provide major services and also succour in time of crises, is both wise and administratively convenient. But there is always a danger of establishing a colony of old people within a town, cut off from proper contact with the other generations, with less and less participation of the next generation in the care of their older people. What is abundantly clear from past experience is that homes and hospitals for old people should be kept geographically distinct and should not be, by implication, just a step from one to the other across a quadrangle. This was the arrangement in the old system of the " house " and the " infirmary," with all its horrors and short-comings. What is needed for an old person who falls ill with anything more than a minor illness is full-scale hospital facilities and diagnostic aids promptly available, not just the doubtful haven of a sick bay without specialist care. Already there are state registered nurses in many welfare homes, next there may be a call for a sick bay—somewhere where these nurses can practise their nursing—and we shall soon be back to the bad old system. Even now there is a tendency for people in welfare homes to develop progressive and remediable disabilities which are not attended to as they might be, simply because they are already " under care " and therefore not a problem of public conscience.

Another unsatisfactory aspect of the present day conduct of welfare homes is the tendency for the residents to have everything done for them in the way of domestic work. For the first time in their lives, perhaps, they are fully waited upon. This may have a very deleterious effect on morale, behaviour and happiness, and perhaps even on their intellectual integrity. No one would advocate forcing the residents to work, but a tradition of participation in chores should surely be established as part of the occupational therapy, which is usually in short supply. In some welfare homes deprivation of incentive can be seen at its worst. The residents just sit, and perhaps do not even think.

The next question to be reconsidered is, who should run the welfare homes of the future, and decide on priorities for admission? At present it is the chief welfare officer often without medical advice, though the family doctor is usually asked for a certificate of fitness for new applicants, and geriatric physicians are available for consultation. If it is accepted that the homes should be for people with manageable disabilities, and if the very high mortality rates amongst the elderly referred to above are understood, there must be a powerful case for the homes being under the overriding control of the geriatric physician for the area, who would also assess the medical fitness of intending residents. A survey of the older, less active people in most existing homes would show how close they are in status to those who are recovering from illness in hospital. Besides, their medical condition must often fluctuate and by this means moves between hospital and home would be facilitated and geriatric expertise would always be available. And if full geriatric department control of policy and admissions were not acceptable policy, at least the homes' medical officers might be required to have special training and to be on the staff of the hospital geriatric department on a part time contract, and the other staff receive proper instruction in geriatric principles. The Seebohm Committee rejected this suggestion on the grounds that the homes would then become less home-like, too " institutional." Anyone who has seen the best new geriatric hospitals with their dayrooms like hotel lounges, need not fear a deterioration in standards. More likely there would be an improvement in the quality of staffing and equipment as the problems of disability became better understood. However not all geriatric physicians, hard pressed as they already are, would welcome the extra responsibility of the residential homes also; their staffs would have to be increased to make this possible, and in particular they would have to have constant advice from social workers as to the non-medical aspects of an application for residential care. Some sort of screening clinic based on a hospital geriatric out-patient department would be a simple means of determining the medical and mental suitability of a person applying to be a resident, for (perhaps) continuing independently after all, with or without suitable domiciliary support, or going to sheltered housing, or in fact going to a residential home (or voluntary home), or to the hospital itself—in the event of major disability and the need for skilled nursing. These are decisions which all geriatric physicians are already taking several times a day in regard to their patients! So, many geriatric physicians see medical control of the " institutional element " of this system as the only logical step in a situation which is rapidly getting out of hand. It follows from this that the administrative and perhaps the financial responsibility for the residential homes would pass to the Regional Hospital Boards or to the Area Health Boards of the future. With this provision, and with the hoped for increase in domiciliary support and sheltered housing, we could foresee a halt to the building of new communal welfare establishments. The existing ones would then become places for the handling of frailty and easily managed disability in an entirely non-clinical atmosphere. Furthermore, in such a system, if the geriatric physician estimated an intending resident's fitness and capability wrongly, he would himself expect to provide the hospital care needed instead, and nothing could be more appropriate. In such a linked system, too, the advantages for all the staff of a better career structure and of a sense of sharing burdens instead of wishing to shift them, as at present, needs no emphasis.

Seebohm and old people: a medical viewpoint

A geriatric physician, made aware every day of the present serious shortcomings in domiciliary services and other social support for older people and their own sad ignorance of what is (or should be) available to them by right, cannot but welcome the Seebohm Report and its insistence on the need for change. The proposed new social service department would undoubtedly ease his hospitals' burdens and provide at last the essential single channel for communication and the calls for aid. His colleagues in general practice must surely agree with this too. But the social service department cannot work well unless there is a substantial increase in the domiciliary services available to old people so that all of them shall be fully available in all areas. But will the social service department, even constituted as proposed, be able to command substantially greater actual resources? Good communications are essential; they will uncover needs, but these cannot be met simply by advice. Only real resources—money, aids, and people with sleeves which roll up —will do this. But will the older people under the care of the social service department get a sufficient share of the resources in face of a demand to relieve the distress of children? The emphasis in the Seebohm Report of family orientation of social work is admirable, but many of the geriatric physician's or welfare officer's clients have only very tenuous family ties, or none at all. There are certainly dangers in the concept of a social service department where all major decisions about old people and their welfare are taken in the context of social work, precisely because the medical content of the problem is so large (*vide supra*). The report, it is true, speaks of the need for close co-operation between the social service department and the geriatric physician or medical officer of health, but there is no obligation, seemingly, for its principal officer to seek medical advice or to listen to it. Many wrong decisions might be taken in this way, and opportunities for prevention and for reducing morbidity and disability lost. There must of course be no question of the social service department being able to arrange the admission of an elderly person to hospital: this must remain, as it is now, a matter to be decided between the patient's own medical adviser and the hospital doctors.

The case for not placing the residential homes for the elderly in the hands of the social service department has been argued above. It is at this point that geriatric physicians see most danger—particularly the risk that the discredited old system might return as the established residents drift gradually into increasing disability.

The logic of placing the responsibility for sheltered housing and special housing for the handicapped solely in the hands of the housing department must also be questioned. The problems in this field are highly complex and are almost entirely medico-social. Recent experience of doctors dealing with major disabilities in trying to get the patient suitably housed does not suggest that this service should remain in the same hands as at present, as the report suggests (para 423).

A geriatric physician, along with pediatricians and most psychiatrists, usually makes, on behalf of his patients, the fullest use of the services provided by local authority departments, with whom he already has daily contact. He is a clinician but he lives in no ivory tower. There are seldom problems of confidentiality (Seebohm Report, para 66) as far as he is concerned, and information flows freely. He can therefore be expected to give the fullest co-operation as the Seebohm Report suggests he should, and to be ready with opinions and advice when asked. He may prefer, for reasons of his own, not to be in the direct employ of the local authority, but this should not preclude him and his department from giving the social service department all the help it requires: this is already an established pattern in many areas. Reciprocal secondment of staff between geriatric departments and local authority departments is also practised in some areas, so the question of what should happen to hospital medical social workers (Seebohm Report, para 689) will perhaps find an acceptable solution. The chance for the geriatric physician to work closely with a colleague of the calibre of the proposed principle officer of the new social service department would be most welcome, but the question must be asked—where will sufficient men of this calibre and experience be found, particularly if the area hospital board is on its way?

8. welfare rights

Tony Lynes

The traditional approach to the problems of poverty is to ask, first, what are the needs of the poor and, secondly, how can those needs best be met. Whether the argument is conducted in terms of the relief or the prevention of poverty, it is essentially paternalistic, concerned above all with what, if anything, should be done for the poor. Recently, however the emphasis has shifted. Disadvantaged groups are seen as potentially able to bring about improvements in their own situation, either by direct action or by pressure on government, both central and local.

So far, there has been a good deal of talk, most of it somewhat theoretical, about community action. The achievements, with a few exceptions, have been more limited. This is not surprising. The poor, as such, are in a weak bargaining position. The circumstances which make them poor also tend to make them powerless. Short of violent protest, just how are the homeless and the slum-dwellers, the disabled and the fatherless, to become a force on their own behalf? Even the low-paid worker is relatively powerless, his industrial situation generally not lending itself to effective organisation—and the record of the trade unions as advocates for their lower paid members has not been particularly inspiring, though the recent pressure for a minimum wage may mark the beginning of a new phase. Without reverting to the old paternalism, it is time to recognise that progress towards social justice can legitimately come through the efforts of middle-class professionals, as well as those of the poor themselves. " Participation " is a fine slogan, but lack of participation is no excuse for inaction.

One of the more hopeful signs of change is the growing tendency to see poverty in terms of the denial of rights. The purpose of this essay is to draw attention to the potentialities of this emphasis on rights as a strategy of social change, but also to point out some of its limitations. One might perhaps describe it as the new Fabianism, in that it seems to offer a means of achieving gradual progress without upsetting the basic value assumptions of our society. The prospects of transforming society's values and priorities into something nearer to a socialist ideal seem to get if anything more distant. Yet, at the same time, it becomes increasingly clear that considerable change in the right direction is possible within the existing scale of values and priorities.

the achievement of rights

There are all sorts of inequalities in our society which are extremely resistant to normal social and political pressures: wage and salary differentials and social class differences in educational opportunity are obvious and crucial examples. Hardly anybody really believes that the labourer ought to be paid as much as the foreman, or the miner more than the managing director—so those who do believe it are in for a fight that will be long or bloody or both before any substantial change occurs in the present pattern of rewards. But there are other kinds of inequality which seem easier to reduce, if not eliminate, because they do not represent a situation which most people believe to be right. On the contrary, once they are aware of the facts, most people can see at once that change is needed, not to over-turn accepted values but, on the contrary, to preserve them. The inequalities to which I refer represent the gap between the rights that people have on paper or in popular belief and what they are able to achieve in practice.

RECOGNITION OF RIGHTS

The American civil rights movement provided the first dramatic illustration of this strategy. The rights it demanded were not new. It sought the full implementation of rights which already existed, which most white Americans already enjoyed, and which were enshrined in the American constitution. For the first time, black Americans began to take white American society at its face value. The civil rights movement did not achieve all its goals. It under-estimated the economic forces ranged against it. But it did certainly achieve a great deal. Above all, it estab-lished a broad based alliance of liberal opinion in favour of radical and relatively rapid reform. But the fact that the reforms turned out to be neither radical enough nor rapid enough does not detract from their importance as an example of what can be done by insisting on rights being made real. " Give us what you admit we are entitled to " is a demand that is not easily resisted.

Legal services for the poor are another example of the strategy of rights ; rights which, in this case, do not yet exist in law, but which do exist in public opinion. There can be little doubt that the growing awareness of the inadequacy of the legal services at present available to—or, at any rate, used by—most working class people in Britain will lead to reform of some kind within the next few years. The right to equal protection by (or from) the law, regardless of income or rank, is accepted without question. When sceptical lawyers like Michael Zander demonstrate that this right, which we have all taken for granted, exists only on paper, nobody argues about whether something should be done. If anything, reform seems likely to be delayed by an excess of proposals rather than by lack of them.

These are cases where rights are clearly recognised and generally accepted, though not fully implemented. But there is another, much more problematic, area of rights to which the underprivileged, or others on their behalf, are increasingly laying claim. A distinction must be drawn between rights that people have *although* they are poor—rights to equal treatment with the better-off members of the community —and rights which people have *because* they are poor. Again we can best illustrate the point by turning to American experience. The civil rights movement, concerned with the achievement by a minority of rights which the majority already enjoyed, inspired the creation of another movement—the welfare rights movement—concerned with rights of a different kind. Across the nation, groups of public assistance recipients, mostly negro mothers unmarried or separated from their husbands, began to demand their " rights " from the local welfare department. Public assistance at certain prescribed standards, they argued, was the right of poor people. They were poor ; therefore, this right must be accorded to them. This was not mere oratory. One of the most remarkable phenomena of the US war on poverty has been the role that lawyers have played in spelling out the right to assistance in precise legal terms, insisting on the publication of local administrative rules and fighting unjust practices through the legal process right up to the Supreme Court. At the grassroots level, the lists of items of clothing and household goods drawn up by the welfare departments as a guide to the standard of material equipment needed by a family have been seized upon by groups of welfare recipients and used in a systematic campaign to extort the last penny from the system by way of special grants for everything from beds to potato-mashers.

The reaction to the welfare rights movement, both among administrators and the public at large, has been less than enthusiastic. After all, what business have these people, whose very existence is a burden on society and whose way of life is clearly immoral, to be demanding their rights? If the rest of us, the decent, hard-working, clean-living majority, are charitable enough to dole out money to these people, should they not be satisfied and grateful for what they get? For, whatever the lawyers might say, public assistance had never been intended as a right—not at least in the sense in which the welfare rights movement was interpreting it. Of course people had a right to be saved from starvation by the application of public funds, though even this right could in practice be limited by what a particular local authority could afford. But to take a list of requirements drawn up for the guidance of social workers in assessing need, and to attempt to translate it, item by item, into a code of legal rights—this was a grotesque perversion of what its authors had intended. To publish such a list, intended solely for the use of the givers of welfare, and to distribute it wholesale to the receivers of welfare, urging them to claim their rights, was to display a fundamental misunderstanding of the system.

The objections to the welfare rights approach did not come only from reactionary administrators and outraged citizens. Many sympathetic and liberal-minded people were deeply worried by developments which, they rightly foresaw, must produce a backlash. If the objective was a more humane welfare system, they argued, the way to achieve it was by making the system more responsive to individual circumstances, by introducing social work skills, and by improving the relationship between the givers and receivers of welfare. The welfare rights movement was doing precisely the opposite: insisting on the legalistic application of regulations and driving the welfare officials into a defensive posture by the threat of legal action if the most trivial rights of welfare recipients were not granted in full on demand. This approach could and did produce short-term results in the form of valuable extra grants for the minority of recipients organised in the local groups—especially in New York. What it could not do was to mobilize a current of public opinion in favour of un-supported mothers on public assistance. It could not do this because the rights on which the movement was based were not generally recognised as such and depended for their validity on the perverse insistence of welfare lawyers that what had been intended as a system of public charity should be administered according to the letter of the law in total defiance of its spirit.

SUPPLEMENTARY BENEFITS

Much the same situation is beginning to develop in Britain. Supplementary benefits, unlike the old national assistance, are a right. The Act says so. But there is a wide gap between the wording of the Act and the spirit in which it is administered. And that gap has very little to do with the viciousness of officials, most of whom are neither more nor less vicious than the rest of us. The fact is that very few people think of supplementary benefits as a legal right in the same sense as wages or even national insurance benefits. Certainly the average British lawyer doesn't. As a result, social workers and others who, in dealing with the Supplementary Benefits Commission, insist on the legal rights of their clients, often get the feeling that they are talking about a quite different scheme from the one the officials are administering. The officials in turn tend to feel that the game is being played accord-ing to rules which they do not accept.

There has, for instance, been a growing demand for the publication of the A Code. This, as is by now widely known, is the book of instructions issued by the Com-mission to its officers at the local level, telling them in considerable detail how they are to use the very wide powers which the Ministry of Social Security Act confers on them. The A Code is not a legal document in the same sense as the Act and the Regulations, which can be enforced in a court of law, or at least before an appeal tribunal. The legal position is, or so it is generally assumed, that an officer of the Supplementary Benefits Commission can deal with any individual case in any way that is consistent with the very wide discretionary powers bestowed on the Com-mission by the Act and Regulations. If, in doing so, he disobeys the instructions contained in the A Code, he may be guilty of a breach of discipline, but not of an illegal act. The victim has no legal redress other than an appeal to the local tribunal, which has the same discretionary powers as the Commission itself and, at least in theory, does not even have access to the A Code. But even if the A Code cannot be legally enforced, it is still true that what a particular individual gets when he applies to the Supplementary Benefits Commission depends just as much on the unpublished rules as on the very general provisions of the Act. Hence the demand for publication—and although that demand has so far rested on arguments about fairness and natural justice rather than on legal rights, some lawyers believe that the courts may eventually compel the Supplementary Benefits Commission to disclose its secret rules.

The official reaction to the suggestion that the A Code should be published has rested on a quite different interpretation of the nature of this document. It is, we are told, a purely internal guide to the officials of the department on the administrative details of their job, and publication of such a document would be a most abnormal procedure. To demand access to it as a matter of right is therefore quite inappropriate. But that is not all. We are also told that publication would not be in the interests of the Commission's clients. The great virtue claimed for the supplementary benefit scheme is its flexibility and the ability of the officers to take account of the particular circumstances of each individual case. The humanity and efficiency of the system rest on the very wide discretionary powers vested in the staff of the Commission. Publication of the A Code, we are warned, would make the system more rigid and less responsive to individual needs.

This is a curious argument. Either the A Code limits the officer's freedom to treat each case on its merits, or it does not. If it does not, then its publication will not do so either. But if the A Code does limit the officer's discretionary powers, then publishing it will not impose any further limitation, except by ensuring that the instructions are complied with. If flexibility is really a virtue, and if the A Code reduces it, then the proper course is to amend the A Code, not to keep it under lock and key so that it can be ignored or deliberately flouted. This is not flexibility. It is anarchy. The real reason for keeping the A Code secret, I suspect, is that supplementary benefits are for the poor and only for the poor. They are a form of communal charity, and the essence of charity is that it is concerned not with people's rights but with their " welfare." To publish detailed rules about the administration of the scheme would conflict with this view of its essential nature. It is greatly to the Commission's credit that it has nevertheless decided to publish a manual for social workers, setting out some of the ways in which its officers are instructed to use their discretionary powers. That it has taken a year and a half to do so since the intention was announced in October 1968 by Judith Hart is perhaps an indication of the difficulty of reconciling theory and practice where the rights of the poor are concerned.

failure of appeals machinery

Similar arguments are used in relation to the supplementary benefit appeals machinery. The Ministry of Social Security Act gives the dissatisfied claimant a right of appeal to a local tribunal, and the Child Poverty Action Group has been concerned to encourage fuller use of this right. The number of appeals heard by the tribunals in the course of a year (some 14,000 in 1967) certainly represents only a tiny fraction of the cases in which the claimant either has been or thinks he has been unjustly treated. But getting people to appeal is only half the battle. Far more appeals are lodged than are actually heard by the tribunals (roughly another 5,000 appeals lodged in 1967 never reached a hearing). Some are withdrawn by the appellant; nobody knows how many or why. In other cases, however, the appellant's benefit is increased or he is given a lump sum grant, and it is assumed that an appeal hearing is no longer necessary, even if the increase is less than what the appellant asked for. He is thus deprived of his legal right to have the tribunal adjudicate on the dispute between himself and the Commission—deprived of it, moreover, by the unilateral action of the Commission. In theory he can appeal against the new decision, but in the vast majority of cases, the appellant gratefully accepts whatever he is offered. The practice of withdrawing appeals in this way, without the appellant's consent, is monstrously unjust and can only happen because the appeal system is seen not as a safeguard of legal rights but as a way of placating dissatisfied applicants.

If the appeal gets as far as a tribunal hearing, the problem arises of ensuring that the appellant is properly represented. The typical appellant appears before the tribunal with a burning sense of injustice but with no idea of what rights, if any, he has. The need for proper legal advice and representation in any proceedings before the courts is fully accepted in principle, if not fully implemented. Yet it is regarded as a positive virtue of the tribunals that lawyers have been kept out of them. Legal aid is still not available for representation by a lawyer at an appeal hearing, and the informality of the proceedings is stressed whenever it is suggested that such representation might be helpful.

The Child Poverty Action Group and a handful of social workers and others have provided skilled representation in a very small number of cases (though enough to show that proper representation enormously increases the chances of success); but most appellants appear alone and unaided, and predictably lose their appeals.

The unspoken assumption seems to be that the tribunals are concerned not with legal rights but with ensuring that the action taken by the Commission is consistent with the welfare of the appellant. There may well be cases in which the welfare criterion leads the tribunal to stretch the law in the appellant's favour. But there are also cases where the paternalist approach of the tribunal leads them to err in the other direction. The wage stop is an example of this. It is intended to ensure that a man will not be better off out of work. Applying the welfare criterion, a tribunal would probably take the view that to reduce a man's benefit in these circumstances is in his best interests, as well as those of the community. Yet wage stop victims who appeal and are properly represented are usually at least partly successful, with the result that they then have a positive incentive to stay out of work. Is it wrong that they should be represented? I do not think so. Most of those affected by the wage stop are men suffering from disabilities which greatly reduce the probability of their finding work, especially with unemployment at its present level. But even if this were not the case, it is surely right and proper that any citizen should make use of the appeal machinery provided by the law and should take advantage of whatever professional or voluntary help is available. If the result of his doing so is regarded as socially undesirable, the proper remedy is to change the law (or the circumstances which lead to its producing undesirable results). In the case of the wage stop, this would mean taking action on low wages and family allowances, so that nobody would be worse off in full-time work than on the normal rate of supplementary benefit. If we are going to argue that people should not have their legal rights because the social consequences may be inconvenient, we would do better to start by looking at the whole field of tax avoidance, in which professional advisers are engaged solely in helping their clients to evade their responsibilities to society.

the rule of law

That the supplementary benefit tribunals are not concerned with legal rights as such is borne out by the fact that they lack one of the fundamental characteristics of the English legal system—its reliance on precedent. This defect became apparent in the recent case of a prisoner's wife who, with the help of the Child Poverty Action Group, won an appeal against the refusal of the Commission to pay her fares for monthly visits to her husband. The policy of the Commission was to pay for visits every two months, despite the fact that relatives are encouraged by the prisons to visit monthly. One might reasonably have assumed that, as a result of this case, the policy would immediately be changed. It was not. The tribunals's findings did not constitute a precedent. If any other prisoner's wife wanted to visit her husband in the " off " month, she would have to go through the palaver of lodging an appeal, and the tribunal might this time decide to uphold the policy of the Commission. Even the woman who won the original appeal could not assume that her fare would be paid in subsequent months. If the Commission chose to stick to its guns, she would have to go back to the appeal tribunal every other month, with no certainty that the tribunal would continue to find in her favour. It was not until four months later that the Commission agreed to pay for visits every month.

To introduce some semblance of legal process into this situation, one would need to establish a higher tribunal or commissioner (as in National Insurance, where an appeal lies from the local tribunal to the National Insurance Commissioner). This higher appeal body would establish precedents which would be binding on the local tribunals. To do this, however, would conflict with one of the basic assumptions underlying the present system: that the function of the tribunal is not to act as a court of law, applying consistent rules to broadly similar situations (like that of thousands of prisoners' wives seeking to visit their husbands monthly), but to look at each case " on its merits," balancing broad humanitarian considerations against a responsibility to the taxpayer.

Once again, as in the case of the A code, the argument is between flexibility and the rule of the law. There are points to be made on both sides. The case by case approach does mean that, if the tribunal is in a warm-hearted mood, it can bend the rules in favour of an appellant. Moreover, the officer representing the Commission at the tribunal hearing may himself be inclined to present the case in a sympathetic light if he feels that the appellant is deserving and unable to argue effectively on his own behalf.

Would all this change if it became the normal practice for appellants to be professionally represented at the appeal hearing? And if so, would the gains outweigh the losses? The question is not easy to answer. There can be no doubt at all that, as things are, the appellant who is well represented stands a much better chance of winning. The success rate for all supplementary benefit appeals is one in five. The success rate for those represented by me is thirteen out of sixteen (no statistics are available for cases where other people have acted as representatives). But if this became general, the Commission would soon take steps to stop the rot. No government department could tolerate its decisions being overruled on appeal in even 50 per cent of cases, let alone 81 per cent. Officers would be specially trained as defence counsel, the hearings would be formalised and there is a risk that the human needs of the appellant would disappear into a cloud of legal jargon. And in the end, the tribunal's decision would often still depend not on questions of law or even of fact, but on its judgment as to the proper application of its discretionary powers to a particular set of circumstances. But at least the appeals system would operate in a reasonably consistent and predictable manner and it would then be possible to use it as a means of establishing clearly defined rights. If a more legalistic approach discouraged the exercise of discretion in favour of the deserving, it would also discourage appeal decisions based on punitive attitudes to those who are apt to be regarded as undeserving: the unemployed, unmarried mothers and so on.

need for open administration

The policy I am advocating, therefore, so far as supplementary benefits are concerned, is one of open administration, publication of rules and administrative practices wherever possible, clear delimitation of the area of decision left to the discretion of the individual officer, fuller use of the appeal tribunals, with skilled representation of appellants, and a two-tier appeals system which would build up a body of case-law. But, in doing these things, we should be aware that we are not merely making the system fairer or more efficient, but changing its nature. It is important to realise this, not only because we must be sure that it is what we really want, but also so that we are prepared for the opposition which such changes in the balance of power in our society are bound to provoke.

LOCAL AUTHORITY WELFARE RIGHTS

Turning to the various different welfare benefits for which local authorities are responsible, one can make much the same points. School uniform grants, education maintenance allowances, rate and rent rebates, free school dinners and welfare foods—these are all examples of that peculiar kind of right which people have by virtue of their poverty. We shall, therefore, expect to find very little emphasis placed on legal entitlement to these benefits or on the use of the legal system to protect such entitlement. And we shall be right in so expecting.

As with supplementary benefits, there is the problem of secrecy. Usually this is not so much a deliberate policy as a failure to recognise that people ought to know what they are entitled to. If a potential recipient asks at the appropriate office, he will probably be given full details of the conditions for claiming a particular benefit —though he should be prepared for several journeys between different council offices before he finally tracks the information down. But if he doesn't take the initiative in asking about his rights, few local authorities will regard it as their responsibility to ensure that he is told about them. And even if he does ask, he will not necessarily be told. There have even been cases of local authority welfare officers themselves being refused information about the income limits for school uniform grants, presumably on the grounds that if they were given this information they might encourage people to apply. The first need, therefore, is for people to be told about their rights — and the advice and information centres recommended by Seebohm, in the unlikely event of their ever coming into existence on more than a token scale, could be an important step in this direction.

But we also need to consider what kind of rights people have to these benefits. There are varying degrees of enforceability. A person who is eligible for a rate rebate, the conditions for which are laid down in an Act of Parliament, can compel the local authority to grant him a rebate. But what about a family which, on paper, qualifies for free school meals? They may be told that the local authority, despite its statutory responsibility, is unable to meet the demand for school meals in its area. The Minister, again on paper, can threaten the withdrawal of grants from a defaulting authority; but, as was found recently when Nottingham withdrew school meals from 2,000 children on a single day, the existence of these powers is no guarantee of their use. And there are other benefits, such as rent rebates, which are not laid down by statute, but left to the discretion of each local authority. What legal remedy is available to a tenant who is refused a rent rebate although apparently entitled to one? Nobody really knows because this is one of the many areas in the field of welfare rights into which the lawyers have yet to penetrate.

quality of service provided

I have discussed the rights of the poor to various kinds of benefits, but the same problems arise in relation to the provision of services—housing, welfare accommodation, education, etc. Here, however, there is an additional complication, in that we are not concerned only with the giving or withholding of a service, but also with the quality of the service. For example, a local authority may accept the responsibility for housing a family, but the accommodation offered may be anything from a roomy, modern house to an overcrowded, substandard slum. In terms of the family's rights (if it has any in this context), the quality of the housing offered may be more important than the mere fact that it has a roof. And all kinds of subtle, or not-so-subtle, discrimination may operate in the allocation of council housing. Do all families have a right to equal choice and equal opportunity in the allocation of different types of accommodation? Morally, I believe they should. Legally, such a right is probably unenforceable—though here again, it remains to be seen what will happen when the lawyers finally move into this area. But, to return to our starting point, in even talking about such rights we are moving far beyond the area which is accepted, by the public and by administrators, as being the concern of the law.

The relationship between the local housing department and its tenants, between the education department and families in need of help to buy school uniforms, between the welfare department and the homeless, are not relationships between equal parties, with rights and responsibilities which can be enforced on either side; they are not relationships freely entered into out of mutual respect. The role of applicant is basically an inferior role and will be felt as such unless a deliberate attempt is made to endow it with the protection of the law. In the whole range of local authority services there is nothing comparable to the supplementary benefit appeal tribunals. There is not yet even a local ombudsman. If the first need is for information about people's rights, therefore, the second is for proper, easily accessible machinery to enforce them.

the need for the definition of rights

The rights of the poor need to be taken more seriously by academic and practising lawyers, by students of social administration and by politicians. The activities of a few gifted amateurs and shoestring pressure groups are no longer enough. There

J

are opportunities here for a concerted attack on some of the most fundamental aspects of social inequality in Britain today. It will encounter resistance, but it starts from a position of strength.

I have not discussed the role of " the poor " in all this; not because I think it unimportant, but because there is so much that can be done without waiting for the emergence in Britain of a welfare rights movement on the American model. Once the under-privileged can see that they actually have rights which can be realised through the legal system, they will find the means of organising to obtain those rights.

9. action for welfare rights

David Bull

Two previous Fabian authors have described the American welfare rights movement and urged the adoption, in this country, of some of its techniques. Ben Whitaker included the Child Poverty Action Group (CPAG) among the four organisations that he saw as the basis for a British movement (*Participation and poverty*, Fabian research series 272, p 19). Tony Lynes in his essay concluded, however, that " there is so much that can be done without waiting for the emergence in Britain of a welfare rights movement on the American model," (p 130). In fact, CPAG has done already far more than can be described here. For instance, the representation of appellants at supplementary benefit appeal tribunals, that Lynes mentioned (p 127), has played an increasingly important part in the work of the Group, which now has a legal department. Unless and until CPAG's proposals for the extension, to social security and rent tribunals of legal aid and advice facilities (Rosalind Brooke *et al*, *A policy to establish the legal rights of low income families*, Poverty pamphlet 1, CPAG, 1969), are implemented, there will be a continuing need, however, for its branches to provide amateur representatives.

These developments are not discussed here; but the suggestions, below, for promoting the fuller use of welfare benefits should be considered in conjunction with not only the Group's welfare law activities, but with proposals to establish neighbourhood legal centres (Whitaker, *loc cit;* Rosalind Brooke, " Civil rights and social services," *Political Quarterly*, vol 40, no 1, January-March 1969, pp 90-102; Michael Zander, " Poverty and the legal profession," in *Unequal rights*, pp 13-16, CPAG and London Co-operative Society Education Department; and Society of Labour Lawyers, *Justice for all*, Fabian research series 273, pp 41-54).

This essay concentrates on only one aspect of CPAG's welfare rights activities: the dissemination of information about a number of means-tested benefits, administered either by local authorities or by the Supplementary Benefits Commission (SBC). It is an account, by a member of CPAG's Manchester Branch, of the branch's experiment to increase awareness of these " welfare benefits." It goes on to examine, particularly in the light of proposals to reorganise the social services and to promote community participation, the various possibilities for the adoption, by statutory and other voluntary organisations, of the branch's approach. Finally, it discusses the value of this strategy, and the dilemmas it creates, for an organisation that is campaigning for the substitution of these *selective* benefits by more *universal* provision.

BRANCHING OUT INTO ACTION

CPAG, formed in 1965 " to promote *action* for the relief, directly or indirectly, of poverty among children and families with children " (my italics), planned to concentrate on increases in family allowances (" Family poverty," *Case conference*, vol 12, no 10, April 1966, pp 331-37). In view of its shoe-string budget, action would have to be restricted to the Westminster-Fleet Street circuit.

During 1967, however, branches began to sprout in the larger provincial cities. Both the Merseyside and Manchester branches aimed " to bring to public notice the existence of child poverty especially in the [local] area; and to *campaign for action* to solve the problem " (my italics). There were no plans for campaigning *in* action. Our main role was to be an *educational* one. By speaking to interested organisations; contributing articles and letters to local newspapers; and by selling *Poverty,* the Group's journal, we could reach an audience that was not accessible to the national office. And through our newsletters and guest speakers, we could educate our own membership.

entitlement campaigns

A few members engaged in social work and teaching were soon asking us, however, to provide another type of information: a guide to welfare benefits. Early in 1968 we began work on such a guide; but then the Minister of Social Security announced her own general entitlement campaign (*Hansard,* vol 760, 4 March 1968, cols 7 and written answers (W)3).

Mrs Hart told CPAG (*Poverty,* no 7, pp 7-10) that her campaign leaflet, *The short step,* would be delivered to 14 million households. It would indicate only " the broad guide lines to entitlement." The Minister did not intend the leaflet to tell people " precisely where they stand in relation to each benefit," but hoped they would " be motivated to make an approach themselves, if they think there is a chance that they might be entitled to a benefit." This made sense, provided that the appropriate officials were capable of handling enquiries from those whose curiosity had been aroused. The leaflet advertised eleven benefits, of which five were administered by the then Ministry of Social Security (MSS), and six by local authorities. It seemed reasonable to assume that the local MSS offices would be prepared for an upsurge in demand; but when we enquired of the 57 local authorities in greater Manchester, few had even heard of the campaign.

information stalls: an experiment

We abandoned plans for our own booklet, and decided to set up, in support of the official campaign, outdoor information stalls. This decision to go out and solicit custom was influenced by our experience with a local constituency Liberal Party. We had contributed, to the party's newspaper, a two-page guide on welfare benefits. The paper, which was distributed throughout the constituency, invited, to any of five public meetings in local schools those who desired more information. A CPAG adviser attended each meeting, but the party officials invariably outnumbered the audience.

We therefore eschewed leaflets and meetings, in favour of making ourselves available where people congregated. We chose a market place and a shop doorway in one of the most deprived areas of the city. It was a modest exercise: on 20 July 1968, a dozen members armed themselves with explanatory literature, and application forms, for ten welfare benefits. A few hand-painted posters were slapped around and we took turns to wear equally makeshift sandwich-boards.

The response exceeded our expectations. In seven hours, more than a hundred people were given forms for benefits to which they appeared to have title. A number had not realised that they were entitled to rent and rate rebates. Most parents were aware of free school meals, yet many of them had not heard of school uniform grants or educational maintenance allowances. Others were amazed at the expenses they were allowed when applying for some benefits, especially school uniform grants and relief from prescription charges.

Five days later, however, the Minister revealed that her campaign would start the following week, but would be restricted to development areas (*Hansard*, vol 769, 25 July 1968, col W215). Our original stall had been opened in support of a nation-wide national campaign; our next stalls in August would help to demonstrate why Mancunians should have received the Minister's leaflet.

We were already worrying lest our activities might appear to suggest that the greater uptake of rights would solve the problem of family poverty, when, to our dismay, a television newscaster took it upon himself to attribute to us a statement of such aims. We decided that, in 1969, we must do more to get across the message that the supplementation of inadequate incomes, by a series of means-tested benefits, is no substitute for a guarantee of adequate incomes, as of right: we would concentrate on family allowances.

family allowances

So we launched our 1969 programme with an address by a distinguished advocate of higher family allowances (Sir John Walley, "A new deal for the family," *Poverty* no 10, pp 9-12). A follow up meeting was held to discuss strategy; but what could we *do*? Eventually, a few branch members interviewed 100 shoppers about their attitudes to family allowances. A majority was in favour of them and doubted that they encouraged either indolence or fertility. Although this made a welcome change from complaints voiced at many of our speaking engagements, neither sample is representative. In telling passers-by about welfare benefits, we acquire valuable evidence against means tests; but even if we asked a thousand of them about family allowances, we would be likely to obtain little new information in support of this universal provision. The government has already the evidence of its own, unpublished enquiry (1968) into the public's knowledge of social security. Even if CPAG had the resources, competing with the Government Social Survey should be a low priority.

Members who feel the fashionable urge to participate in a survey can be accommodated by something like the Manchester Post Office Survey (D. G. Bull, "Out-of-form Post Offices," *ibid*, no 12/13, pp 10-12). This demonstration of the obstacles to low-paid workers obtaining welfare benefit forms attracted considerable publicity. We sought no publicity, on the other hand, for our token gesture to involve branch members in the fight for family allowances; 1969 was another welfare rights year.

Although we did not intend to run information stalls, on three occasions we did so. At the request of a Methodist minister, we paraded our wares, on two June Saturdays, in a busy, Salford street. We also operated at a jumble sale in his church. Although roadside custom was as hectic as ever, only two people were helped at the jumble sale. This setback, plus our earlier experience with the Liberals, and discussions with our York colleagues who had leafletted 10,000 households and held special follow-up "surgeries," which attracted only ten people (Jonathan Bradshaw and Richard Bryant, *Report on a welfare rights information stall*, mimeographed, CPAG, 1969), should have warned us to reject the minister's invitation to join him in the church each Friday evening, to answer further enquiries. Nevertheless, we accepted. After three weeks and one enquiry, we gave up.

We should certainly have known better than to accept, in October, an invitation from the National Council for Civil Liberties (NCCL), to co-operate in a weekly advice centre in the Moss Side area of Manchester. Leaflets were distributed and the local People's Association published, with our help, fortnightly features on welfare rights in its newspaper; but all previous experience suggested that we would be wasting our time.

student action

There was, however, a new factor to be considered: a student section of the local branch had been formed in the Manchester University Union, and wished to concentrate on welfare rights. With youthful optimism, the students agreed to participate in the NCCL venture. Having interviewed half a dozen visitors in two months, they decided to go in search of custom, and successfully established another roadside stall. Meanwhile, along with a few other members and an occasional helper from a Citizens' Advice Bureau (CAB), the students had manned a mobile information office in support of the city council's own welfare rights venture. This involvement with the corporation is only one of the developments that caused us to become much more of a welfare rights agency in 1969.

becoming a welfare rights agency

It was perhaps inevitable that we would have to take on an advisory role, although we had vowed not to become involved in any visiting of families. We had hoped to take a few names and addresses of people who were willing to be interviewed by the mass media, and to refer less straightforward problems, with the permission of the people concerned, to the appropriate office. Otherwise, we planned to distribute application forms to those who preferred to take them home, but to complete most forms on the spot. Although most people were surprisingly willing to forget their shopping and stand at the roadside discussing their finances, few forms could be completed there: some housewives had little idea how much their husbands earned; and, anyhow, corroboration of earnings was required for most benefits. We had to trust that most people would be able to complete the forms at home, but undertook to follow up some of the most complicated cases.

We were already beginning to be looked upon as an advisory agency, though, before we set up information stalls. Publicity in the local press had resulted in letters from people requiring help; and social workers were referring problems to us. Our stalls merely served to establish us as consultants on welfare benefits. Our main welfare rights involvements in 1969, however, were with the city council and with the mass media.

working with the city council

In February 1968, Manchester City Council instructed the Town Clerk to convene " immediately on receipt of the report of the Seebohm Committee," a meeting of the relevant corporation officials and representatives of appropriate voluntary organisations, in order to examine the existing arrangements for " the early detection of the effects of poverty in Manchester families " and for their " obtaining assistance of all kinds." The meeting would be asked to suggest " ways and means of improving public awareness of entitlement to available benefits."

A year later, seven months after the Seebohm Report (*Report of the committee on local authority and allied personal social services*, HMSO, 1968) had been published, the meeting was convened. Delegates received a comprehensive memorandum which included various suggestions for improving the council's administration of its welfare benefits. For instance, a factual handbook of welfare benefits might be prepared; and an explanatory leaflet could be distributed to every home in the city.

Nine voluntary organisations, including Manchester CPAG, assembled before the meeting and welcomed both proposals. They urged that the distribution of the leaflet take the form of a campaign: professional advice should be obtained on the design of the leaflet; the support of the mass-media must be sought; campaigns should be mounted in selected areas of the city; and a mobile information office could be used, as the campaign progressed from one area to another. It would also be necessary to make arrangements at the Town Hall: there should be a central information desk which would have all relevant forms and would direct callers to the appropriate offices; while the relevant staff would need to be made aware of all the available benefits, so that applicants for a particular benefit could be told of other help to which they might be entitled.

At the subsequent meeting, a working party was established, to prepare the leaflet and the handbook. In August 1969, the City Council voted £1550 to produce and distribute 300,000 copies of the leaflet, plus £200 to defray any losses on a handbook to be published by the local Council of Social Service. No provision was made, however, for establishing a central information office: the officials felt that the city's Publicity Office could take on this additional responsibility. The relevant chief officers were asked to make their departments aware of the benefits outlined on the leaflet; but this exercise was hampered by the officials' insistence that the distribution of the leaflet commence in September 1969, although the CAB and CPAG representatives argued that the officers would first need to have copies of the handbook. No public relations man was engaged: the language used was, for the most part, that of the CAB and CPAG representatives who drafted the leaflet. This was, in some ways, encouraging, although the education official insisted on translating, into official language, the section describing his committee's benefits. Nor would he tolerate any mention of his committee's discretionary schemes for essential clothing and for travel passes for children who live too near to their schools to qualify automatically.

It was agreed to phase the distribution of the leaflet; but a campaign office was thought unnecessary: the authority "must leave some scope for individual initiative." As a compromise, the CAB and CPAG representatives undertook to man a mobile office. Unfortunately, they were given only a weekend's notice that distribution was about to begin. Then, unwise choices of sites probably contributed to the poor attendance at this office; but only a dozen people turned up on a site where a hundred had used our information stall. By inviting people to climb the steps and enter the caravan, we appeared to have introduced a barrier from which our stalls had been free.

The mass media received the same inadequate notice. Yet the case for seeking their support, in not simply reporting the campaign but in advising on the benefits, had been agreed by the working party. The task had been entrusted to the city's Publicity Officer; it was left to us, however, to negotiate belatedly, and not very successfully, with the media.

wooing the mass media

This was not a new experience for the Manchester branch: like the Group's national office, we had become increasingly busy during 1969, suggesting advisory features to the mass media or eagerly responding to requests to assist with such items. ITV companies have been especially ambitious: Granada led the way with an 18-week series, *This is your right*. The Manchester CPAG chairman wrote briefs for the seven features on welfare benefits. Thames followed with a similar series, written and presented by the Group's welfare lawyer. Both programmes were transmitted in the early evening, unlike the BBC's *Plain man's guide to his welfare rights*, which was broadcast in mid-afternoon on Radio 4 (25 September 1969), when few plain men will have been tuned in. Plain housewives may be expected to benefit, however, if *Woman's hour* can find the time for more advice on " Yours by right," such as that given by CPAG's Director in a couple of programmes in autumn 1969.

There must be even more scope, surely, for series in newspapers, especially local ones; but when we suggested to editors of 37 local weeklies that they might feature, during Mrs Hart's campaign, benefits available locally, only one responded. When *The short step* campaign failed to reach Manchester, this paper produced a five-week series to coincide with our stall in its locality. The leading local evening paper originally brushed aside suggestions for such features, but a new editor, in September 1969, enthusiastically welcomed the idea. He felt that such articles would only be meaningful, however, if they were topical. Accordingly, an article on rate rebates was published a fortnight before the October closing date for applications; but the November changes in the scales for supplementary benefits and free school meals passed unnoticed.

IMPROVED PUBLICITY: FUTURE PROSPECTS

We have had a slight influence, then, on the approach to welfare rights by one of the 57 local authorities in our area, and, in a modest way, have shown that the mass media have an untapped potential for helping the authorities. The educational task ahead of us is clearly beyond us. The next two sections of this essay examine the prospects of a take-over of our activities: how can official publicity and the contribution of the mass media be improved; and what are the implications for social work and advisory agencies?

Considering the policy of " pottering around with posters and playing at public relations " (Howard Glennerster, *National assistance: service or charity?*, Young Fabian pamphlet 4, p 10) that it inherited, the Labour government's publicity for welfare benefits at first appears encouraging. Its Ministry of Social Security Act of 1966 marked a new emphasis on the " right " to a means-tested benefit, and £48,220 was spent on advertising this new deal for pensioners (*Hansard*, vol 760, 5 March 1968, col W72).

Yet CPAG had fought, that summer, a losing battle to achieve better official publicity for rate rebates (Tony Lynes, " Rate rebates: what went wrong?", *Poverty*, no 1, pp 10-12). If the Minister responsible for this " case-study in non-communication " (*ibid*, no 3, p 14) is exaggerating when he describes his publicity as " continuous since 1966 " (*Hansard*, vol 760, 4 March 1968, col W22), at least rate rebates are advertised at the beginning of each half yearly application period. Publicity needs to be concentrated, however, not only at appropriate times but also on particular groups.

The Minister has promised, for instance, " to get the scheme more widely known, especially among tenants paying inclusive rents " (*ibid*, vol 758, 9 February 1968, col W256). The percentages of council tenants and other indirect ratepayers receiving rebates in 1968-69 were 2.7 and 2.3, respectively, compared with 6.7 per cent of owner-occupiers and other direct ratepayers (*Rate rebates in England and Wales 1968-69*, HMSO, 1969, p 66). Yet the percentages in the previous year were 2.7, 2.4 and 6.7, respectively (*ibid* 1967-68, cmnd 3725, HMSO, 1968, p 67); it seems that the Minister's unapparent efforts have had the results they deserved.

Similarly, changes in supplementary benefit scales are advertised; but new scale rates mean that the definition of low income, for the purpose of claiming relief from NHS charges, is altered too. This fact is not advertised. Nor is it likely to be, so long as the Minister of State is unable, or unwilling, to grasp this point (*Hansard*, vol 793, 15 December 1969, col W210). Modifications in the scales for school meals should be advertised too; but while the Department of Education and Science remained dazzled by the response to the £20,000 worth of letters that children took home in the autumn of 1967 (*ibid*, vol 758, 8 February 1968, cols 626-27), a repeat performance seemed unlikely. Even an announcement of a further increase in price (*ibid*, vol 791, 17 November 1969, cols 861-64) brought no mention of a new publicity drive, but following pressure by MPs (*ibid*, vol 793, 11 December 1969, col 618) the DES promised (circular 4/7c) a further letter to parents.

The government's earlier enthusiasm for rights campaigns has evidently waned. The demise of Mrs Hart's plans is a sad symbol of this. The official explanation of the restriction, to development areas, of the door to door distribution, was that the take up rate in these areas could be compared with that in regions where the leaflet was distributed through social service agencies, or not at all. CPAG is sceptical: if the Ministry was really running a controlled experiment, " it would surely not have selected all the poorest regions for the first stage, thus invalidating any comparison with the rest of the country " (*Poverty*, no 8, p 3). Perhaps " Treasury meanness " upset Mrs Hart's plans (*ibid*, no 10, p 16)? Or perhaps SBC officers objected to the additional burden of enquiries?

Whatever the reasons for it, the limiting of the campaign to special areas made impracticable a nationwide publicity campaign. Moreover, the Minister successfully put the press off the scent by sending them in search of the workshy. Six months earlier, she had instigated a special enquiry, as a result of the publicity given to " several examples of young men apparently living on supplementary benefit and making no attempt to find work " (*Annual report of the Department of Health and Social Security for the year 1968*, cmnd 4100, p 251, HMSO 1969). Whether the results of this investigation justified her subsequent schemes for terminating the supplementary benefits of some unemployed men has been discussed elsewhere (*Poverty*, no 9, pp 1-4); what matters, in the present context is that the Minister chose to announce these schemes in the very collection of written answers in which she revealed that her entitlement campaign would start soon. Mrs Hart must have known that, by demonstrating her awareness of " obligations " as well as of " rights," she would not pacify those newspapers that had caused her enquiry; they would concentrate on her workshy campaign and spend the silly season in search of sensational cases. If one considers this with Mrs Hart's enthusiastic account of her plans (*Poverty*, no 7, *loc cit*), one realises how any attempt to launch an official campaign is at the mercy of politicians and officials who may wish to suppress information about rights.

political delay and official conservatism in Manchester

Manchester's official campaign suffered similarly. The original resolution, moved by our then vice-chairman, with the support of his Labour fellows, was easy prey for an irrelevant Conservative amendment that delayed action until the Seebohm Committee had reported. This political manoeuvre wasted a year: action on welfare benefits had to await not only the publication of the Seebohm report, but the council's deliberations on it.

At first, the progressive memorandum appeared to have been worth waiting for; but it soon became clear that this represented the commitment of an official from the Town Clerk's Parliamentary Office, whose campaigning zeal failed to infect some of his colleagues. If we had been responsible for the leaflet, the education department's discretionary benefits would have been included; distribution would have been postponed until the booklet was ready; the co-operation of the mass media would have been sought in creating a "campaign;" and the movements of the mobile office would have been advertised in the leaflet and synchronised with its distribution.

Yet we could never have afforded to print the leaflet and distribute it to every home in the city; some branches have exhausted their limited funds with much less ambitious leafletting ventures. It seems wasteful, though, to distribute so furtively £1550 worth of leaflets. An official analysis has revealed an increased uptake of only one benefit: chiropody. Significantly, this service is free for all elderly or disabled people.

The failure to campaign is especially disappointing in Manchester, where informal methods of taking information to people are far from new to the city council. Housing officials have visited clearance areas in a caravan (D. G. Bull, " Housing departments and clearance areas: problems of communication," *Social and economic administration,* vol 2, no 4, October 1968, pp 250-70); and Manchester was the first education authority to open an " education shop," following the ACE experiment " to test the supposition that educational advice and information could be put across to a working class audience if it was given in everyday instead of official surroundings " (Lindsey March, *The education shop,* p 3, Advisory Centre for Education, 1966). The dilution of the original proposals for a rights campaign is a further reminder that the enthusiasm of a few councillors and officials cannot jolt a whole bureaucracy into innovation.

potential of the mass media

If the mass media are to do more to publicise welfare benefits, much of the initiative will have to come from those who administer them; yet most of the local press reports of Mrs Hart's campaign appear to have been inspired by CPAG branches (personal communication from the Department of Health and Social Security). We have certain advantages over the administrators in attracting the attention of the media: we can reveal administrative shortcomings and can often furnish examples that demonstrate these or other problems. On the other hand, officials should be able to accumulate more information on popular misconceptions about welfare benefits; and working full time, they really ought to stimulate more reports by the media than CPAG volunteers have been able to manage.

While the promotion of reports should achieve more than advertisements alone, advisory features are necessary too. There is support, from within, for the media to assume an advisory role. *New Society* (" Observations," 23 October 1969) has argued, for instance, that " far greater use could be made of television as an educative medium. More satisfactory information about the existence of rights and of means of obtaining them is the necessary prologue that must come before all other action." And in a TV discussion that followed a film of our efforts to provide such advice (*The Persuaders*, BBC 1, 11 February 1969), Mr David Kingsley, the ad'man, regretted that " newspapers and television [had] not used more the responsibility . . . they have in order to explain the facts of legislation and people's rights, as well as commenting on them."

It might be argued that radio's *Can I help you?* has been doing this for 30 years. A birthday tribute (*Radio Times*, 9 October 1969) praised this programme's handling of " the common problems of humanity." Most of the problems appear to be especially common, however, to middle class listeners, who are surely more likely to tune in to " the reassuring voice of a lawyer, accountant or insurance expert," or some other exponent of BBC-English. It seems a pity that the more exciting and vernacular approach of *A plain man's guide* (the guide to welfare rights was only one in a too occasional series) cannot be offered regularly and at a time when more plain men are listening. Since it is the plain housewife, however, who will usually negotiate to obtain the family's welfare rights, it is to be hoped that *Woman's hour* will maintain its interest in this field. The inability of most plain men to receive a VHF message thwarted Merseyside CPAG's plans to publicise benefits on local radio. The decision to allow transmissions on medium frequencies should open up a new channel for communicating rights.

Television has obvious advantages over radio, in the size of its audience and in the presentation of its message. On the other hand, the lack of visual variety was one of the factors that limited the items on welfare benefits in *This is your right*. The TAM ratings exceeded expectations, however, and Granada is hoping to overcome the presentation problem in a further series.

Few newspapers have exploited their great advantage in this field: readers can re-examine difficult points and check back-copies. Some popular Sundays do offer advice, of course, to those readers who write for it. The John Hilton Bureau of the *News of the World* deals, each year, with " two and a half times as many cases as the whole legal profession put together " (Zander, *op cit*, p 15), and no consumer organisation receives as many complaints (Lucy Syson and Rosalind Brooke, " The voice of the consumer," in Brian Lapping and Giles Radice, eds, *More power to the people*, p 64, Longmans 1968).

There is a need, however, for more *unsolicited* advice, on a regular basis, or at least when it is topical. The *Sunday Mirror* is occasionally " At your service " with such advice. Only nationally uniform benefits can be covered adequately in the national press; there is considerably more scope for local newspapers. Four out of five electors regularly read a local newspaper (Committee on the management of local government, *Management of local government*, vol 3, p 29, HMSO 1967).

Yet Merseyside CPAG found that rate rebates were the only welfare benefit for which the press was the main source of information (Peter Moss, *Welfare rights project '68*, p 18, Merseyside CPAG, 1969). The local press had published advisory features as well as advertisements, but most rating authorities in greater Manchester consider the latter to be the most effective method of publicising these rebates (Jennifer Dale, *Rate rebates: study of a selective scheme*, unpublished BA Econ dissertation, University of Manchester, 1969, p 43).

Manchester CPAG has persuaded only two local editors that there is a potential for advisory features; but since the authorities seem disinclined to encourage such publicity for their benefits, we will have to go on wooing editors and feature writers. However enthusiastic their response, this could be of limited value so long as journalists continue to see those who qualify for welfare benefits as either " the poor " or as scroungers. The reporter who refused to ask a low paid worker why he did not claim free school meals for his two children, because " he had four pints of milk and a television set," was a particularly frustrating example of the first failing; but we have encountered repeatedly journalists who are interested in failures to claim only if they cause *" real hardship."* Such reports might win the sympathy of the wealthy, but they may well deter those who find it difficult to manage on weekly incomes around the £15-£20 mark; a family in this bracket should be interviewed instead, so that hundreds more like them, as well as those who are even worse off, might become curious about their own rights. We have usually fought a losing battle on this score, although one BBC producer has recognised that while *shocking* the complacent rich may be the goal of a feature on poverty, a discussion of welfare benefits should invite *identification.*

This will remain an elusive goal while reporters hunt the workshy. Even accurate reports on this subject must add to the stigma involved in claiming welfare benefits; all too often, however, reporters suggest that these benefits are the prerogative of the unemployed. In such a complex field, one must expect mistakes of the non-specialist journalist. More newspapers should employ social services specialists. Convincing a few editors of their responsibility to advise may be of little avail, so long as most newspapers are incapable of reporting accurately on welfare benefits.

INTERPRETERS AND MEDIATORS

Adrian Sinfield concludes, in his essay, that the roles of the social worker include those of " interpreter and mediator for the citizen " (p 58). It was to help them in the first capacity that social workers asked us to prepare a guide to benefits. There can be little doubt of the demand for such booklets. The Liverpool Personal Service Society launched the first local guide to *Welfare benefits* in 1968; and York CPAG, and subsequently other branches, followed suit. Three thousand copies of *A guide to national welfare benefits* (Poverty pamphlet 2, CPAG) were sold, to social service agencies, within a month of its publication in December 1969. Preparation for this role should start earlier, CPAG suggested to the Seebohm Committee: social workers should " be trained as givers of information " (Memorandum of evidence; summarised in *Poverty*, no 3, p 14).

The Group argued that " social workers have to spend a great deal of time helping families to disentangle themselves from complex financial situations which need not have occurred had they known of the available sources of help in time." Some social workers, in asking us for information about benefits, have emphasised that they spend too much time checking them, at the expense of those who need their traditional skills.

a limited role for the social worker

Better informed social workers might spend more time, however, in mediating on behalf of clients who experience difficulties in claiming benefits. By appointing Tony Lynes, a non-social worker, to its children's department, Oxfordshire has obtained a consultant whom its social workers can approach on these matters, as well as an intermediary and a representative at tribunals. We have been used in this way in Manchester. Some social workers merely expect us to reach a higher level of authority than they would normally approach. Others wish to conceal their identity: local authority social workers have complained, for instance, that senior officers have vetoed their requests to the SBC, for their clients to be told, in writing, how their benefit was calculated; or they fear that their good relationship with a local office may be impaired if they, themselves, tackle the problem. These restrictions and inhibitions are not peculiar to Manchester (*ibid*, no 5, p 2). Moreover, social workers may be particularly tempted to opt for the preservation of amicable working relationships, especially with the local SBC manager, if the client is " undeserving."

These restrictions are only one reason why better-informed social workers have only a limited part to play in the promotion of welfare rights: many eligible families will never come into contact with them. There is clearly a need for a neutral organisation that will go out to find those families and support them in any consequent disputes with those who administer welfare benefits.

a role for Citizens' Advice Bureaux?

Can CABX fill this bill? A CAB organiser who visited one of our stalls expressed surprise at the steady stream of enquiries: why hadn't these people gone to her bureau, just round the corner? There could be several answers. We tell many callers of " problems " they never knew they had; and others know of benefits they might have claimed, but would never have thought of asking a CAB how they might obtain them. Some approach us out of curiosity; others may be waylaid. Even a well advertised, well situated, modern bureau, with long opening hours, such as that of the organiser in question, cannot expect to compete with a casual roadside stall. People in clearance areas have made good use of informal offices (Bull, " Housing departments and clearance areas: problems of communication," *op cit*); but a more vigorous attempt to solicit custom is necessary when the service in question is the object of not only ignorance and miscomprehension, but of stigma, too.

It is hardly surprising, then, that CABX have received few enquiries from people enquiring about welfare benefits *per se*. It might be supposed, however, that some of those with " financial and material needs " would be advised of their entitlement to these benefits. Clients who fall into this category account, together with those who require advice on supplementary benefits, for about a tenth of the visits to Manchester CABX. Since most of them have deeper problems, however, the CAB workers do not explore their welfare rights, but refer them to the appropriate social work agencies.

If CABX are to take over from us, they must change their approach. Sinfield hopes they can " make themselves better known to the public and more accessible, with longer opening hours and often better-placed and more attractive offices " yet feels there are " strong grounds for experimenting with the community shops that appear to have been one of the more successful parts of the American action programme " (p 54). But although the advocates of the " consumer shop " whom Sinfield cites in support of his argument, doubted whether CABX " could be improved enough " (Syson and Brooke, *op cit*, p 73), Rosalind Brooke has subsequently argued that the bureaux " are admirably suited to provide the base for an expanded service for people to be told their rights and to be helped to obtain them " (" Civil rights and social services," *op cit*). She stresses, however, that this will depend on their forgoing their policy of " impartiality and non-campaigning." Similarly, the Labour Party's National Executive Committee finds inappropriate the CAB's " almost entirely neutral role " and suggests that bureaux should " play a more positive role in promoting equality of access, and should receive Government aid on a wider scale " (*Labour's social strategy*, p 80). But would such government financed advisers be any more independent than statutory social workers?

a community work solution ?

The Seebohm Committee evaded such issues and was content to quote the warning, from the Council for Training in Social Work, that local authorities would " need to recognise the fact that some of its staff may be involved in situations which lead to criticism of their services " (para 494). Alternatives should have been examined. Robert Holman (" The Wrong Poverty Programme," *New Society*, 20 March 1969) not only questions whether community workers employed by local authorities would have sufficient freedom, but fears that voluntary organisations dependent on the financial support of local authorities would be hamstrung. Anne Lapping (" Social Action," *ibid*, 12 January 1969), considers the possibility of a central agency's employing community workers but anticipates conflict between such a service and those of the local authority.

Helping people to claim their rights is one of the aims of the government's community development project that Holman describes. In the circumstances that he and Anne Lapping discuss, however, community workers might become little more than walking guidebooks. Perhaps the authorities would settle happily for this, but community work implies that catalysts will encourage people to open up their own channels of communication, which will remain open when they move on. Some feel that CPAG should be the catalyst that would enable the poor to unite in a fight for their welfare rights. This feeling is particularly strong in the York branch (Mary Cooper, " The humiliations of poverty," *Poverty*, no 10; and R. Bryant, *Do the poor need us?*, unpublished paper to CPAG conference, 19 October 1969). Tony Lynes concludes that " once the under-privileged can see that they actually have rights which can be realised through the legal system, they will find the means of organising to obtain these rights " (p 130). Yet, it could be that, people who suddenly obtain perhaps an extra £3 or so in benefits might prefer to rest content, rather than let the whole neighhourhood know why and how they obtained that money. Those who urge community action in this context sometimes fail to distinguish " between rights that people have *although* they are poor—rights to equal treatment with the better-off members of the community—and rights which people have *because* they are poor " (p 121, Lynes' italics).

Similarly, Marris and Rein have observed that " to be poor is not itself a status which defines a common political interest. It is, rather, a humiliating condition which most people are ashamed to acknowledge, and from which anyone with the ability to lead has also the ability to escape " (Peter Marris and Martin Rein, *Dilemmas of social reform*, pp 185-6, Routledge 1967). Bryant argues that this assumption is " heavily conditioned by class conceptions of leadership and organisational skills " and that a greater handicap is " non-access to those material and informational sources that middle class pressure groups naturally tend to command ": it should therefore be " one of the central roles " of CPAG branches to provide such resources. Militant groups like the Manchester Anarchists and the local Community Research and Action Group, which have sought our help in the preparation of rights leaflets, appear to take this optimistic view. So did the community association that invited us to address its members on welfare benefits. There

K

was a good turn out, but the discussion was dominated by demands to remove tinkers from cleared land in the area.

This was a community issue; welfare rights are a personal matter. We should not expect people to attend meetings on welfare benefits or to participate in any other activity where they have to stand up and be counted as persons in need. The York school argues that CPAG branches should use their welfare rights projects to find potential leaders for activities that *do* affect a community. One of the aims of the weekly information stall that York CPAG established in the local market (Bradshaw and Bryant, *op cit*) was to provide " a focus of discontent felt by the poor in their dealings with officials " (J. R. Bradshaw, *Welfare rights: a strategy of social action*, unpublished).

councillors: a neglected channel?

Councillors may feel that *they* are fully capable of assisting the poor in such dealings and of providing information and advice. Moreover, the government argues that the creation of local government ombudsmen would reinforce the councillor in the performance of these two roles: he would be able to " help a citizen in a case where no maladministration has occurred, for example by drawing his attention to some benefits for which he can apply or by pursuing his case with officials " (*Reform of Local Government in England*, cmnd 4276, para 85, HMSO 1970). A reform that forces elected representatives to learn more about the services provided by their councils is to be welcomed; but are we expecting too much of these overworked amateurs? Councillors in Manchester clearance areas had difficulty in interpreting policy and appeared to over estimate the part they played in disseminating information (Bull, " Housing departments and clearance areas: problems of communication," *op cit*). Not surprisingly, most people preferred first-hand information from officials. In expressing fears that " consultation and participation . . . could lead to a by-passing of (the) locally elected representatives " (City of Manchester, *Report of the general and parliamentary committee*, August 1969, para 37), the city fathers appear oblivious to what is happening already—and not only in Manchester: official enquiries have shown that the electorate prefers to consult " the town hall "—or its equivalent. (*Management of Local Government, op cit*, vol 3, ch 2). It would be optimistic to envisage a significant role for councillors in advising on welfare rights.

the work-setting

Perhaps more could be done to advise men in their work setting, since low paid workers make inferior use of their welfare rights, compared with recipients of supplementary benefits (MSS, *Administration of the wage stop*, para 18, HMSO 1967;

MSS, *Circumstances of families*, paras 67-69, HMSO 1967; *Poverty*, no 2, p 3; no 4, p 25; and no 6, pp 11-13).

The recruitment, by employers, of experts on the social services is not unknown; but this may often be by accident, rather than design (Barbara N. Rodgers and Julia Dixon, *Portrait of social work*, pp 199-202, OUP 1960). There is ample scope, too, for improvement in the advisory services of trade unions (*Poverty*, no 5, p 3); but many of those workers who most need advice seem unlikely to be members of unions (Society of Labour Lawyers, *op cit*, p 27). Although he acknowledges this limitation, Richard Bryant hopes that CPAG will " encourage Trade Unions to become involved in what in America is called social unionism—that is unions sponsoring programmes to promote and protect their members' interests in the community as well as in the place of work."

It seems more desirable, however, that CPAG concentrate on lobbying the support of the unions for increased family allowances and an incomes policy that favours the lower-paid.

a door to door service

The National Suggestions Centre (NSC) has experimented with a mobile advisory service on rights (John Baker and Christopher Cross, *The Newham experiment*, NSC, 1969; summarised in " Taking the rights to the citizens," *What?*, summer 1969). During a weekend in June 1969, a " mobile canvassing team " visited 198 households and discovered problems in more than half of them.

The NSC commends its technique to local authorities and other agencies " who ... want to uncover the hidden part of their welfare iceberg;" but few authorities seem very anxious to find those who do not claim their welfare benefits. How much more *should* they be doing to develop the approaches tried by the NSC and ourselves? Can our experimental methods be institutionalised?

AN OFFICIAL TAKE-OVER?

Baker and Cross estimate that, with a paid interviewer, an operation like theirs could be run " for well under £200." Even at £100—or 10s a household—this would clearly be beyond the various voluntary bodies mentioned above. Moreover, the expenditure would not stop there. The NSC found, as we did, that distributing the appropriate forms is only a beginning: a follow up revealed that many families had failed to act on the advice they had been given. It must be recognised that some people will fail to claim even if their rights are explained fully and only a signature is required of them (see, for instance, Ministry of Pensions and National Insurance,

Financial and other circumstances of retirement pensioners, para 90, HMSO 1966): the pride and independence of the potential recipient is an inherent obstacle to the full take-up of means tested benefits.

Means tests are not efficient as a way of concentrating help on those in need. They are rationing devices which favour the more articulate and uninhibited; and those who can penetrate bureaucracy and complete forms, or who are in touch with someone who will help them to do so. For reasons stated at the outset, it is not intended to expand on that issue; we must be content to discuss what should be done to maximise the possibility of everyone's knowing his rights and to help people claim means tested benefits. The CPAG and NSC experiments have underlined the need for authorities to improve, in this context, in at least two ways: their services must be more accessible and they must make more home visits.

accessibility

Despite the clumsy and diffident attempts by central and local government to become more communicative about welfare rights, it does not seem unduly optimistic to assume that the combined effects of the recent spate of official reports and of papers both white and green must include a considerable improvement in the information about, and access to, the social services. No doubt, the very thought of " participation " will send tremors through the corridors of town halls as it did when the Skeffington report (Ministry of Housing and Local Government, *People and planning,* HMSO 1969) was considered in Manchester (City of Manchester, *op cit*); and as *Shelter* has found, in one London borough (Des Wilson, " Crusade in chains," *The Guardian,* 11 February 1970), the actuality may be such participation as the council will tolerate and can direct.

It is not so much the Skeffington Committee's interest in *participation* as its proposals for improving *information* that should concern us here. We have observed already, however, that an openness on the part of one department is no guarantee that others will be so keen to communicate with the public; in urging planners " to go out to the people to inform them " (para 20), the committee was preaching to the comparatively converted. Perhaps other departments *will* heed, though, the recommendations for " imaginative posting " (para 170). The sites suggested include bingo halls, pubs and launderettes; Merseyside CPAG recommended launderettes and chip shops (Moss, *op cit*, p 26).

Expressing concern about inaccessibility, the *Royal Commission on Local Government in England 1966-1969* (cmnd 4040, para 317, HMSO 1969) endorsed the Seebohm Committee's recommendation (*op cit*, paras 588 and 680) of area offices. Of more specific interest in the present context, perhaps, is the latter's allusion (para 108) to the desirability of employing, in these offices, area information officers. CPAG had in mind information centres to be located near, but clearly separated from, the social workers' office: " the function of the information service is not to act as a mouthpiece for either central or local government, but rather as a deliberately created ' ombudsman-service ' (Memorandum to Seebohm Committee, *op cit*). The service would not be part of the social work establishment, but would provide information for it. The service " must also be capable of taking information out into the neighbourhood rather than merely dealing with callers." Experiments like the " education shop " and slum clearance enquiry offices have been noted; and the London Borough of Lambeth has recently sent a mobile information office into shopping centres (*What?*, Autumn 1969, p 30). We have not been optimistic about any early spread in these approaches; but perhaps we should invite officials to help at our stalls? In the autumn of 1968, senior education, rating and SBC officers provided very useful information stalls for social workers and others attending our welfare rights conference; but would they let their juniors face the public at the roadside?

more home visits

There is, of course, another way in which the officials could go out to the public: by knocking on their doors, as the NSC suggested. This could mean knocking on every door; on those in selected areas; or the doors of those who had asked for help, either for a particular benefit or in some other way. The first approach is obviously necessary if authorities are to achieve even the limited end of ensuring that everyone receives an adequate explanation of his rights; but financial considerations will inevitably restrict door knocking to areas where need is imagined to be greater. Otherwise, there are various sieving devices for determining who receives home visits. The approach of the SBC is an instructive example. True, it might be advertised more vigorously that *any* communication will bring a visitor, and many post offices could do more to spread that message (Bull, " Out-of-form Post Offices," *op cit*). Once a claimant has made contact, however, a home visit is arranged (unless otherwise requested); and in theory (*Administration of the wage stop, op cit*, para 41), if not always in practice (*Poverty*, no 6, pp 6-7; and Dale, *op cit*, pp 58-62), SBC officials should tell claimants, in certain circumstances, of other benefits available to them.

This is, of course, costly: twelve times as many officials are needed to administer supplementary benefits for two and a half million claimants as are needed to operate family allowances for four million families (Barbara N. Rodgers, " A new plan for social security," *New Society*, 17 October 1968). Yet local authorities should have similar responsibilities. The Secretary of State for Education had the right idea when, in his autumn 1967 letter, he invited parents of schoolchildren to request a home visit. But the welfare hawks thought this unwise (*Hansard*, 8 February 1968, *loc cit*); and EWOs complained to us of the strain on their service. Significantly, when Manchester Education Committee sent parents, in May 1968, an ambitious, if incomprehensible, explanation of its benefits, all enquiries were handled centrally. This was disappointing, since the EWO service is a medium through which a greater uptake of benefits could be promoted. Mr and Mrs Butcher are a case in point:

On his wage of fifteen pounds a week, Mr Butcher was clearly entitled to free school meals for his six children, a school uniform grant for the child at secondary school, and rent and rate rebates. Yet when he and his wife called at our information stall, they were receiving just one free school meal. We gave them the necessary forms and said we would call in a few weeks' time. By then, an EWO had visited, in response to the Butchers' application: all six children were now getting free meals, and the eldest had been awarded a uniform grant. Neither parent had been able, however, to complete the rent and rate rebate forms. We helped them do so, and they now pay the rent man 11s less each week, and have received a rate rebate worth 12s 6d a week.

This family was visited by a corporation official whose job it was to administer a means test. Should he not have satisfied himself that the Butchers needed no other benefits? They not only required help to complete rent and rate rebate forms; we subsequently advised them about free prescriptions and, when we learned that Mrs Butcher was pregnant, about free welfare foods. A whole hearted attempt to make means tests effective would entail periodic revisits of existing claimants.

If EWOs are not expected to check other entitlements, considerably less help can be expected from those departments which make no home visits and have no " welfare " functions. Some rating officials feel uneasy about encouraging the use of rate rebates, let alone other benefits (Dale, *op cit*, p 66).

Seebohm and Redcliffe-Maud

Although the social service department, as envisaged by the Seebohm Committee, would have brought together the administration of education means tests and those for home helps, meals on wheels and laundry services (para 601), rent and rate rebates, the other two local authority benefits in which we are mainly interested, would remain the responsibility of at least one other department. Indeed, outside county boroughs, they are the responsibility of another tier of authority. The proposals of the Royal Commission on Local Government would have brought into common authorities the relevant functions—assuming that the *administration* of rent rebates would be treated, in metropolitan areas, as a function of district council housing management, and not of upper tier rent policy-making. In short, the proposals would have brought means tests for education and certain welfare benefits into one department and into the same tier of authority as rate and rent rebates.

In its subsequent *Local Authority Social Services Bill* (1970) and local government White Paper, however, the government has different ideas. For instance, education welfare is not to be a statutory responsibility of the social service committee. The Home Office Minister of State has explained that while it " could not mandatorily switch the whole of this sphere [of education welfare] to the personal social services without enormous difficulties arising . . . about the statutory requirements in regard to child attendance," the government is " open-minded about the possibility of this [department's] case work . . . coming under the direction of the director of the social services " (*Hansard,* vol 796, 26 February 1970, col 1518). The same applies, presumably, to the department's means tests; but the government's decision to make education an upper tier responsibility (*Reform of Local Government in England, op cit,* para 22) could possibly hinder the carve-up, in metropolitan areas, of education welfare powers. Rating, too, is to be an upper tier function (para 23).

In metropolitan areas, in other words, the district councils will administer benefits that are used mainly by the aged, and, if the above assumption regarding housing management be correct, rent rebates too. Rate rebates, on the other hand, will be the responsibility of the upper tier authority, as will education means tests, unless it is thought practicable to transfer them to the lower tier's social service department.

It is *not* being suggested that the government should have taken into account such considerations. It seemed necessary to indicate, however, that although they will reduce greatly the number of unique means tests that local authorities operate; will bring them into all purpose authorities throughout most of the country; and will concentrate a number of them into a new department, the proposed reforms of local government and of the personal social services will not result automatically in a streamlining of local authority means tests.

This should not preclude, however, the appointment of visitors responsible for local authority means tests: if the SBC can administer means tests for benefits available from local health authorities and executive councils, why could not the social service committee appoint a visitor whose responsibilities, in metropolitan areas, might include means tests for benefits administered by another tier of authority? Or perhaps the SBC should administer more local authority means tests?

The Seebohm Committee alluded to the " major issue of principle " whereby direct financial help to people in need is largely a prerogative of central government, then proceeded to give two confusing examples (paras 603-4), which appeared to illustrate the case for a widening of the SBC's scope, to include, for instance, the administration of education maintenance allowances. Yet the committee concluded merely that the social service department might need emergency powers to assist financially those households where only adults are involved. But, of course, there are arguments against the SBC's administering local authority means tests. Its responsibility for NHS benefits must help to engender the belief that these are exclusively for SBC recipients; or is it simply that the SBC has a greater stigma than have local authorities? Whatever the reason, the evidence mentioned above, on the uptake of benefits by low wage earners, suggests that those administered by the SBC are most under used. In view of its recruitment problems, it would hardly be practicable to charge the SBC with new responsibilities; and it would be naive to assume that assessment clerks made redundant by local government reorganisation will transfer to the SBC. Organisational difficulties must not be made an excuse for a failure to rationalise means tests. More can be done to facilitate joint applications for rent and rate rebates; and we should not meet, as we have done, recipients of free school meals who are unaware of other education benefits. Governments can reorganise and rationalise, but cannot legislate against a lack of imagination.

a continuing role for CPAG ?

That pessimistic conclusion suggests that there will remain ample scope for CPAG to participate in the promotion of welfare rights. Even when local government ombudsmen arrive, there will remain a need for outside bodies to which those who dispute their judgments may turn. Moreover, it is difficult to imagine officials adopting some of our unorthodox techniques.

Nor can we be confident that CABX will remove quickly their own barriers to communication; and are they identified, anyhow, as part of the official machinery? The possibility of CPAG's being seen in the same way may increase if and when local authorities do more to publicise welfare benefits, since we could find ourselves working even more closely with them, in order to fill the remaining gaps. This is only one of the dilemmas that face us, in deciding whether welfare rights stalls are a proper activity for a group that advocates more universality.

A PRESSURE GROUP'S DILEMMA

While it is not uncommon for a social service pressure group to " seek to persuade partly by example " and to provide a service as " a means of promoting a cause politically " (Allen Potter, *Organised groups in British national politics*, pp 37, 156, Faber 1961), the peculiar paradox of our activities is that we are helping people to use a system to which the Group objects. So, while we may feel pleased that our experiment *could* help to indicate what is needed of the authorities, we have been concerned that our activities might reinforce and appear to condone the present system.

The advantages to our members of our maintaining a liaison with the relevant authorities have been described above; again, it is not uncommon for pressure groups to act as intermediaries for their members (*ibid*, p 172). The Birmingham Claimants' Union told a CPAG conference, however, that we should remain more aloof: it is tactically unwise, for instance, to approach officials by telephone. Yet when a phone call, from Mr Jim Radford, the "anarcho-syndicalist" leader of the London squatters, to the chairman of the GLC housing committee, is partly responsible for 2000 empty houses being made available to the homeless (*Observer*, 12 October 1969), we can take heart. While he recognised that such official support "might be considered the kiss of death," Mr Radford affirmed, realistically, that he was "not opposed to working with anybody who wants to help the homeless."

Another champion of the homeless has argued that the pursuit of short-term gains can produce longer term results: "The pressure group believes that meeting some need is better than meeting no need at all, and that often tackling need directly is the most effective way of gaining both the experience and the credibility to bring about change." (Des Wilson, "The power and the pressure," *The Guardian*, 27 January 1970). Our information stalls can be seen in this more optimistic light: our "customers" have benefited; so have our members; and, despite our anxieties, our basic aims must have been furthered in some directions. It would be difficult to persuade families who are a pound or two better off each week, as a result of visiting our stalls, that we should have concentrated on family allowances. Moreover, those who advised them have learned more about welfare benefits, and social work members have been able to implement knowledge gained at our stalls.

Although the relevance of welfare benefits to solving family poverty is sometimes misunderstood, it would be a pity to withdraw, for this reason, from activities that have enabled us to inform on four fronts: our information stalls offer opportunities for educating both the member and, literally, the man in the street; and they provide evidence for our arguments with both the government and the taxpayer.

If our welfare rights strategy is "the new Fabianism, in that it seems to offer a means of achieving gradual progress without upsetting the basic value assumptions of our society" (p 120), then our four pronged attack seems to depart from the Fabian tradition of influencing élites. Moreover, organisations that have mocked our gradualism have sought our help in advising on welfare rights. After all, we never promised a revolution; we merely attempted a lawful demonstration of people's rights. The message has not been entirely lost on the local authorities and the SBC; but the difficulties we have encountered, and the burdens we have acquired, suggest that the authorities are unlikely to accept full responsibility for making means tests effective. CPAG must continue to be means tests watchdogs.

conclusions

The conclusions that have been drawn, in the above evaluation of a local experiment, have excluded, for reasons stated at the outset, any solution in terms of the abolition of means tests. Yet if means tests are here to stay so too is stigma. Efforts to present them as " rights " may make selective benefits more acceptable, but methods that ask those in need to stand up and be counted seem unlikely to succeed.

While improved publicity may encourage more people to seek their rights from the appropriate authorities and to consult the traditional advisory services, the need for claimants to present themselves will remain a serious barrier to access.

Our approach, and that of the NSC, overcame this barrier. So much following up of difficult cases and checking with officials is required, however, that our method cannot be made efficient, on a regular basis, by a group of volunteers. This is another reason why CABX seem ill equipped to relieve us of these burdens. And the authorities responsible for welfare benefits seem unlikely to go to such lengths to make selectivity effective. The reorganisation of social services and of local government offers opportunities for improved administration of these benefits, although there could be difficulties in metropolitan areas. Organisational problems cannot excuse, however, inefficiency that arises from a lack of imagination. Nor should the promotion of welfare rights be seen as a social work exercise; it is a much larger public relations task.

We have demonstrated that the mass media seem prepared to provide considerably more help in furthering this cause than the authorities have sought of them. It would be naive to assume, however, that the media will not continue to hinder the administration and utilisation of welfare benefits by their often biased, and invariably misleading, coverage of abuse.

Indeed, while administrators and politicians, along with the media and their consumers, continue to be so emotionally disturbed about a small minority that abuses the welfare state, it will be up to CPAG to go in search of those with a right to help.

index